DEADLY DARLINGS

THE HORRIFYING TRUE ACCOUNTS
OF CHILDREN TURNED INTO KILLERS

MURDER AND MAYHEM SERIES #2

WILLIAM WEBB

Absolute Crime Press
ANAHEIM, CALIFORNIA

ABSOLUTE CRIME

www.AbsoluteCrime.com

Contents

ABOUT ABSOLUTE CRIME

Absolute Crime publishes only the best true crime literature. Our focus is on the crimes that you've probably never heard of, but you are fascinated to read more about. With each engaging and gripping story, we try to let readers relive moments in history that some people have tried to forget.

Remember, our books are not meant for the faint at heart. We don't hold back--if a crime is bloody, we let the words splatter across the page so you can experience the crime in the most horrifying way!

If you enjoy this book, please visit our homepage (www.AbsoluteCrime.com) to see other books we offer; if you have any feedback, we'd love to hear from you!

Sign up for our mailing list, and we'll send you out a free true crime book!

http://www.absolutecrime.com/newsletter

Dear reader, your heart may not be able to handle the shocking true facts presented in this humble volume. You have been warned.

INTRODUCTION

We all know that murder is among the most terrible crimes a person can commit. Understanding and coping with murders committed by adults can be extremely difficult for even the most intelligent people.

But when a child commits murder the crime becomes all the more terrible because it challenges our most basic ideas of innocence and humanity.

Even seasoned law enforcement professionals, judges and prosecutors have a difficult time dealing with killer kids. Yet murder committed by children is not as rare as you might think. Children are capable of every kind of crime including robbery, sexually motivated killings and even child murder.

The savagery of children rivals and sometimes exceeds that of adult killers.

Read on, and you will see a viciousness that makes the Lord of the Flies look like a Boy Scout gathering.

Alyssa Bustmante:
Teenaged Thrill Killer
and Church Goer

Introduction

Ignoring violent behavior on the part of children and teenagers is not a good idea. Most violent criminals, including many serial killers, get their start torturing and injuring animals, or worse, other children when they are kids. Many of them exhibit violent behavior long before they graduate to killing.

A typical example was Alyssa Bustamante, a 15-year-old Missouri girl who had been talking about, and in some cases, faking violent acts long before she slit her nine-year-old neighbor's throat. This case proves that not doing anything about violent behavior or talk of violent behavior on the part of a child or teen can prove fatal.

The Thrill Killer Next Door

In some ways, Alyssa Bustamante was a normal teenaged girl; she liked writing in her diary, using Facebook, and going to church in her small town. Yet she was also a monster who stabbed and slit the throat of her nine-year-old neighbor.

The writings and photographs in Bustamante's journal and posts on her Facebook page reveal that she was a real life Jekyll and Hyde, even though she looked like a normal teenager. Yet she was constantly writing about killing others and even planned to kill some of her classmates at the local high school. Alyssa also put on bizarre makeup to make herself look like a Death Metal singer or a serial killer.

Pictures from the journal also show Bustamante about to stab a boy with what looks like a hunting knife while another boy holds him down. YouTube videos she posted online show her attempting to electrocute her own brothers.

A Day off from School Leads to Murder

On Friday, Oct. 17, 2009, Alyssa Bustamante had the day off from school. She spent part of her time off digging two graves in the woods near her house. Alyssa used the graves on Oct. 21, 2009 when nine-year old Elizabeth Olten disappeared.

Bustamante saw Olten, her neighbor, walking home and grabbed her off the street. Alyssa then beat and stabbed Olten before slitting her throat. Once she was done with Olten, Bustamante buried her in one of the graves she had dug in the woods.

Incredibly, Bustamante then went home and wrote in her journal that killing was an amazing and pretty enjoyable experience. Then, like a true psychopath, Bustamante headed off to church. Since it was Friday night, Bustamante was probably attending a youth group. Obviously she wasn't a very devout Christian, even if she was a regular church goer.

A Mysterious Case and Did Alyssa have Help?

There are some mysteries about the case; Alyssa apparently did a good job of hiding the body. Authorities were unable to find it in their initial search, even though they were led to the right location by the GPS in Elizabeth's cell phone. The search party might have walked right over the body.

Instead, detectives were led to Alyssa Bustamante by a mysterious letter that fingered her as the killer. This sounds like Alyssa either had help burying the body or showed somebody else where it was. Her accomplice or friend then turned her in with an anonymous letter.

When investigators finally confronted Bustamante, she confessed to the crime and led them to the body. How police were able to get her to confess is not known, but they might have already had evidence.

One disturbing possibility is that somebody who may have helped Alyssa commit the murder got away with it. Authorities might be covering for the other person in order to protect a child's anonymity.

The Violent Monster in Plain Sight

One really frightening aspect of the case is that Alyssa Bustamante had a long and well documented history of violence and psychiatric problems long before the case. Pictures of her pretending to stab other teenagers with a knife and video of her encouraging her own brothers to touch an electric fence are posted online.

Alyssa even listed her hobbies as "killing people" and "cutting" on her YouTube account. She was apparently the one who posted the video where she tried to get her brothers to touch the electric fence and get hurt on YouTube. Violence also runs in Alyssa's family; at the time of the murder, her father was serving a 10-year prison sentence for assault.

Bustamante was also apparently under the care of a psychiatrist or psychologist at the time of the murder. Testimony at court hearings revealed that Alyssa was taking the psychiatric drug Prozac at the time of the crime. The drug apparently did not help her and may have contributed to her crimes.

Did Prozac Turn a Teenaged Girl into a Killer?

At court in Jefferson City, Mo., Alyssa Bustamante pled not guilty to first degree murder. Her attorneys then attempted a very unusual defense that partially worked. They tried to blame her murderous behavior on the psychiatric drug Prozac.

An expert named Dr. Edwin Johnstone testified that Prozac and other similar drugs can cause murderous behavior in some people. This wasn't the first time Prozac has been blamed for a teen murder; in 2011, in the Canadian province of Manitoba, Judge Robert Heinrichs ruled that Prozac caused an unidentified teen to stab 16-year-old Seth Ottenbreit to death. Prozac's manufacturer and the Canadian government disputed the testimony that convinced Judge Heinrichs to make the ruling.

Bustamante pleaded guilty to second degree murder and was sentenced to life in prison without parole in 2011. The testimony prevented a trial in the case. Interestingly enough, news articles indicate that Missouri state law might enable Bustamante to get parole and walk free at some point because she was not sentenced as an adult.

Her case was aided by the judge, who ruled that part of her diary could not be entered as evidence at the trial. The judge may have thought that the journal entries and pictures of the girl might prejudice the jury against her.

Alyssa Bustamante Today

Alyssa Bustamante is currently serving her sentence in the Missouri state prison system. Even though she's eligible for parole, she'll probably never receive it. It's doubtful that courts will release her without some sort of appeals court ruling.

Despite the claims that it can cause murderous rages, Prozac, or flouxetine, which changes the chemistry of the brain, is still widely prescribed. Only time will tell if the Bustamante case is an isolated incident or a warning about the potential side effects of a drug.

Bibliography

CBS News Staff. "Alyssa Bustamante Picture Gallery at 48 Hours website ." n.d. cbsnews.com. Online Picture Gallery and Commentary . 13 February 2013.

Crimesider Staff. "Alyssa Bustamante called 9-year old girl enjoyable then went to church." 6 February 2012. cbsnews.com. Online News Blog. 13 February 2013.

drugs.com. "Prozac ." n.d. drugs.com . Online Database Entry . 13 February 2013.

Fenske, Sarah. "Alyssa Bustamante: Prose-cutors Can't Use Part of Killer Teen's Confession." 23 June 2011. blogs.riverfronttimes.com . Online News Blog . 13 February 2013.

Monacelli, Antonia. "Murderous Children: 15 Year Old Alyssa Bustamante Brutally Murdered a 9-year Old Girl ." 8 February 2012. antonia-monacelli.hubpages.com . Online Encyclopedia Entry . 13 February 2013.

Newcomb, Alyssa. "Teen Thrill Killer Alyssa Bustamante Could Get Paroled Today ." 8 February 2012. abcnews.go.com . Online News Article . 13 February 2013.

Turrene, Paul. "Teen murder case hinges on Proazac ." 4 August 2011. torontosun.com . Winnipeg Sun newspaper Article reprinted in Toronto Sun . 13 February 2013.

LIONEL TATE: AMERICA'S YOUNGEST KILLER

Introduction

Convicting a child murderer can be difficult because courts and laws are not designed to deal with such a case. Even seasoned prosecutors can have a tough time getting a stiff sentence for such a killer. When they do succeed it can be tough to make the sentence stick because case law has few precedents for such a crime. The prosecutors' job is often made tougher by the huge amount of media attention such cases generate. A classic example was the case of 12-year old Lionel Tate. There was ample evidence to show that Tate had brutally beaten a six-year old playmate to death, yet his conviction was later overturned on appeal.

The 12 Year Old Murderer

Lionel Tate was the youngest person ever to be sentenced to life imprisonment in the United States. His crime was a bizarre one that might have been an accident in which Tate, then 12, beat a six-year-old girl named Tiffany Eunick to death.

Tate's trial become controversial and a media circumstance because of some sensational claims made by his attorneys. The attorneys claimed that Tate was mentally incompetent and incapable of telling the difference between professional wrestling and reality. They also tried to implicate America's most popular professional wrestler, Dwayne "the Rock" Johnson, in the death.

Did Wrestling Cause a Little Girl's Death?

The tragedy began on July 28, 1999 when Lionel's mother Kathleen was asked to look after Eunick, a friend's daughter. Kathleen made dinner for the kids, then left them downstairs alone to watch TV. She went upstairs to sleep and didn't check on the two.

Around 10:40 p.m., Lionel went upstairs and got his mother. He told her that Tiffany wasn't breathing. When Kathleen came downstairs, she found that Tiffany's body was already cold. Ironically enough, Kathleen was serving as a Florida State Trooper at the time of the murder.

Lionel told his mother and the court that he was merely imitating wrestling moves he saw on TV. Professional wrestling, especially violent extreme wrestling, was booming in the U.S. at the time, and like many young boys, Lionel was a huge fan. His favorite wrestler was the ultra-violent Dwayne Johnson, a.k.a. the Rock, who was then the main attraction of the World Wrestling Federation, or WWF (now WWE). The defense was that Lionel was a simpleton who couldn't tell the difference between fantasy and reality.

The Evidence Tells a Different Story

The evidence told a very different story. An autopsy showed that Tiffany had suffered a violent beating that lasted over five minutes. Among other things, she had a broken rib, a cracked skull, and severe damage to her liver and kidneys. Her body was covered with bruises. The evidence showed that Tate had savagely beaten Tiffany rather than wrestled.

In 2001, Tate was put on trial for the crime, and the defense introduced the wrestling defense. They even tried to subpoena professional wrestlers such as the Rock to appear, but their efforts were rebuffed. The wrestlers never appeared in court, even though rumors that subpoena servers were looking for the Rock, who lives in Miami, were floating around on the internet at the time.

Tate was eventually convicted of first degree murder and sentenced to life in prison. The jury simply didn't buy the claims that he was only playing.

He only Served Three Years

Even though he was sentenced to life in prison, Lionel Tate ended up serving only three years in prison. In 2003, an appeals court threw out his conviction because he wasn't given a mental competency evaluation before the trial. Since Tate had already served three years in prison, he was ruled eligible for parole.

Tate was able to leave prison in January, 2004 because the state of Florida decided not to retry him. Perhaps prosecutors wanted to avoid another media circus. Even though Tate wasn't free, he didn't remain that way for long.

Back Behind Bars

Tate's subsequent actions showed that the claims that he wasn't very smart might have been true. In Sept. 2004, he was arrested with a knife in his hands outside his house, a clear parole violation. In 2005, Tate was arrested for armed robbery of a pizza delivery man at gunpoint.

This time, Tate faced 30 years in jail for violating his parole. Once again, he tried to claim that he had mental problems and even claimed that he was hearing voices. Tate's attorneys tried a number of ploys to win his release, including a demand for a brain scan. The judge in the case didn't buy the claims and sent Tate back to prison to serve his full sentence.

Psychologists who examined Tate found that he was competent and trying to feign incompetence. A letter that was presented as evidence of his mental illness was shown to be a forgery, possibly created for Tate by other inmates in prison.

Lionel Tate Today

Lionel Tate is still in prison serving the full toll for the 2005 parole violation. He was convicted of robbing the pizza deliveryman in 2008. Tate, who is still in jail, maintains his innocence and even claims he was framed for the robbery. He occasionally gives interview in an attempt to get his side of the story out to the media.

Even though he maintains his innocence, Lionel Tate's stories are hard to believe. In 1999, he was three times the size of Tiffany Eunick, who weighed just 45 pounds. Lionel was nearly six feet tall and weighed 166 pounds at the time of Tiffany's death.

The truth is that despite all of his claims to the contrary, Lionel Tate savagely beat a little girl to death for no real reason. Since then, his behavior shows that he is a self-serving liar and possibly a sociopath who will probably spend the rest of his life behind bars.

Bibliography

ABC News . "Leniency for Lionel Tate ." n.d. abcnews.go.com. Online News Article . 13 February 2013.

Anglefire.com. "What WE Do to Our Children ." 9 March 2001. Anglefire.com. Wire Service News Article . 12 February 2013.

CBS 4 I-Team. "I-Team: Lionel Tate Talks from Behind Bars." 22 September 2011. miami.cbslocal.com. Online News Article. 12 February 2013.

Kennedy, Kelli. "Young Killer is Ruled Competent; Lawyers Acknowledge His Ruse ." 20

December 2005. nytimes.com . NY Times News Article . 12 February 2013.

Monacelli, Antonia. "Murderous Children: 12 Year Old Lionel Tate Killed Six Year Old Girl." n.d. antonia-monacelli.hugpages.com . Online Encyclopedia Article . 12 February 2013.

New York Times . "Articles About Lionel Tate ." 12 February 2013. topics.nytimes.com . Archive of News Articles . 12 February 2013.

BARRY LOUKAITIS: MIDDLE SCHOOL GUNSLINGER

Introduction

School shootings are among the most frightening and disturbing of crimes. These events are particularly horrific because they involve people who target unarmed children with powerful weapons. Such tragedies are often made worse because the perpetrators are usually children themselves who target their classmates. Another reason why such shootings are frightening is that their causes are poorly understood. One of the most frightening school shootings was carried out by Barry Loukaitis, who turned his father's gun collection on his classmates and his algebra teacher. The disturbed Loukaitis, dressed in a black overcoat (or duster), may have been an inspiration to the Columbine high school shooters who also dressed in black overcoats for their rampage three years later.

Gunslinger in the Classroom

In the 1990s, a number of school shootings turned American classrooms into killing fields. School shooters imagining themselves as modern-day gunslingers took aim at bullies, teach-

ers, classmates, and other perceived torment-
ers. One school shooter, Barry Loukaitis, even
dressed up as a gunslinger before going on the
rampage.

Like a gunslinger, Loukaitis armed himself
with a rifle and two pistols. He even used a
longcoat called a duster to conceal his weapon,
just as gunfighters sometimes did in the Old
West. Then he walked into his algebra class
and started shooting. The reasons for Loukaitis's killing spree are unknown, but his horror
was soon overshadowed by the greater horror
and tragedy of the Columbine High School
shootings in Colorado.

From Troubled Teen and Dysfunctional Family Member to School Shooter

Barry Loukaitis was an honors student from a troubled clan that seemed to be a textbook example of the dysfunctional family. His father, Terry Loukaitis, was a distant man who cheated on his mother. His mother, Joann Phillips, responded by speaking of suicide and threatening to force Barry to commit suicide as well.

Joann Phillips's bizarre behavior may have helped inspire her son's murderous rampage. Some reports indicate that she was threatening to commit suicide on Valentine's Day in 1996, two weeks after her son's killing spree. Her suicidal behavior was reportedly becoming worse in January 1996.

Barry apparently suffered from mental problems and was reportedly taking Ritalin and other psychiatric drugs. If that wasn't bad enough,

Loukaitis was also bullied at school, particularly by a boy called Manuel Vela, who supposedly called Barry a fag. Barry himself claimed that bullying drove him to kill his classmates.

Rage in Algebra Class

Nobody knows why Barry Loukaitis chose Feb. 2, 1996 for his shooting spree, although the rampage itself indicates he was planning it for some time. That morning, Loukaitis dressed in his black duster and took three guns that belonged to his father. The weapons were a 30-30 caliber hunting rifle (a deer rifle), a 347 caliber pistol, and a .25 caliber semiautomatic pistol. He also brought along 78 rounds of ammunition.

To avoid being detected on the school bus, Loukaitis walked to Frontier Middle School in Moss Lake, Wash. Once at school, he went to his fifth-period algebra class and interrupted his teacher, Leona Caires, by shooting her. After gunning down his teacher, Loukaitis reportedly said, "This sure beats algebra, doesn't it?"

He then opened fire on the panicking students, hitting four of them. Two of the students, Manuel Vela and Arnold Fritz Jr., were killed. Another student, a girl named Natalie Hintz, was shot in the chest and right arm. Her arm had to be amputated because of the wounds she received.

Gym Teacher to the Rescue

Loukaitis then tried to take the students hostage, but a heroic gym teacher named Jim Lane came in and saved the day. Lane first volunteered to be a hostage in place of the students. Then when Barry was distracted, Lane tackled him and subdued him, ending the nightmare.

Did Pearl Jam Made Make Him Do It?

Barry Loukaitis was only 14 years old at the time of the shooting. He was also apparently mentally disturbed, which made his trial into a blatant media circus. The carnival-like nature of the crimes was amplified by the media references.

Prosecutors claimed that Loukaitis took inspiration from a Pearl Jam song Jeremy, Stephen King's novel Rage, and two movies, Natural Born Killers and The Basketball Diaries. They noted that Loukaitis quoted from Rage after shooting Caires and attacked his algebra class just like the main character in the book.

The trial was delayed because a court appointed psychiatrist named Joan Petrich was asked to examine Barry's mental health. Petrich testified that Loukaitis was delusional, had mood swings, and felt like God during the shooting. In September 1997, a jury in Seattle found Loukaitis guilty of two counts of first degree murder, one account of second degree murder, one count of attempted first degree murder, and 16 counts of aggravated kidnapping. He was sentenced to 205 years in prison without parole.

The Reasons Why are Still Unknown

The reasons for Barry Loukaitis's killing spree are still unknown. Barry suffered from mental illness at the time of the shooting; he had been diagnosed with hyperactivity and clinical depression. Loukaitis was taking the drug Ritalin (or methylphenidate) for hyperactivity at the time of the shooting.

Psychiatric drugs have been blamed for the behavior of other teenaged killers, including Alyssa Bustamante, who was taking Prozac when she slit her neighbor's throat and buried her in the woods. Like Prozac, Ritalin affects chemicals in the brain. It is known to impair thinking and reactions.

The known side effects of Ritalin include aggression, restlessness, and hallucinations, so it is not far-fetched to assume that the drug Barry Loukaitis was taking to control his hyperactivity caused his murderous rampage.

The Tragedy Continues

Barry Loukaitis is serving his sentence in the Washington State penal system; news reports indicate he is at the Callam Bay Corrections Center. His attempt to get a new trial was rejected by the Washington Supreme Court in

1999, so it is likely that Loukaitis will die in prison.

Loukaitis's actions may have also caused another mass shooting. Ten months after the Frontier Middle School shootings, Aaron Harmon, the cousin of one of Loukaitis's victims, Arnold Fritz Jr., shot and killed his mother, his sister, and himself. Some reports indicate Harmon was depressed because of his cousin's death. Arnold's father, Phil Fritz, later shot himself at his son's grave. So Barry Loukaitis may have claimed more victims, even though he was behind bars.

Bibliography

Blanco, Juan Ignacio. "Barry Dale Loukaitis
." n.d. murderpedia.org . Online Encyclopedia
Entry and Compilation of News Articles . 14
February 2013.

CBS News Staff. "Alyssa Bustamante Picture
Gallery at 48 Hours website ." n.d.
cbsnews.com. Online Picture Gallery and
Commentary . 13 February 2013.

drugs.com . "Ritalin ." n.d. Online Database
Entry . 14 February 2013.

Fenske, Sarah. "Alyssa Bustamante: Prosecutors Can't Use Part of Killer Teen's Confes-

sion." 23 June 2011. blogs.riverfronttimes.com

. Online News Blog . 13 February 2013.

Fitten, Ronald K. "Loukaitis Jurors Hear

Parents ." 9 September 1997. murderpedia.org

. Seattle Times News Articles . 14 February

2013.

—. "Moss Lake Teen Guilty In 3 Murders -

Jury Rejects Notion Loukaitis Insane ." 4 Sep-

tember 1997. murderpedia.org . Seattle Times

Newspaper Article . 14 February 2013.

Geranios, Nicholas K. "Wash. marks anni-

versary of school shooting ." 2 February 2006.

boston.com/news. Associated Press Wire Ser-

vice News Article . 14 February 2013.

Wikipedia . "Columbine High School Massacre ." n.d. en.wikipedia.org . Online Encyclopedia Entry. 14 February 2013.

Wikipedia. "Frontier Middle School Shooting." n.d. en.wikipedia.org. Online Encyclopedia Entry. 14 February 2013.

CRAIG PRICE: 15-YEAR-OLD SERIAL KILLER AND WARWICK SLASHER

Introduction

In most cases, legal technicalities and loop-holes help child killers walk free. There's one notorious child killer, Craig Price, the serial killer known as "the Warwick Slasher," who has been kept in prison because of such technicalities.

Incredibly, Price is not serving time for the three murders he committed when he was 15 and the murder he committed when he was 13. He only served five years in reform school for those crimes in which he stabbed a mother 60 times and her two young daughters 30 times in their own home. Instead, Price is serving 25 years in prison for assaults on prison guards and a contempt of court charge that comes from his refusal to undergo a court-ordered psychological evaluation.

A Serial Killer on the Rampage

In 1989, the people of Warwick, R.I. were horrified to discover that a woman and her two daughters had been stabbed to death. The crimes bore an eerie similarity to Richard Ramirez's Night Stalker rampage in Los Angeles. As in that case, somebody had entered a home and committed a brutal murder. The fears were compounded by the similarity to another murder of a woman two years earlier.

What residents didn't know was that the murders had been committed by a 15-year-old boy. A boy who had started killing when he was just 13 two years earlier, a boy named Craig Price. Nor did residents suspect that the case would generate controversy that exists to this day.

A Grisly Discovery by a Grandmother and a Sister

Warwick's nightmare began on Sept. 4, 1989 when Marie Bouchard and her daughter,

Mary Lou Bouchard, came to check on Joan Heaton, who lived in the Buttonwoods area of Warwick. Heaton was Marie's daughter and Mary Lou's sister. The two were worried because they hadn't heard from Joan or her two daughters for days.

When they entered the home, the two discovered that the inside of the house was splattered with blood. Worse, they soon found the bodies of Joan Heaton and her two daughters, 10-year old Jennifer and 8-year old Melissa. All three had been stabbed to death with knives probably taken from the kitchen. Melissa had been stabbed with such force that a broken knife was found in her neck. An autopsy indicated that Joan had been stabbed 60 times and the children 30 times.

Police believe the murder had been committed three days earlier during the Labor Day weekend. They and residents noted the similarity to another murder two years earlier, that of Rebecca Spencer, who had been stabbed to death in her living room with a packing knife. Like Joan Heaton, Rebecca Spencer had been stabbed 30 times.

A 15-Year-Old Suspect

It isn't exactly clear what led detectives to suspect Craig Price, a 15-year-old boy who lived in the neighborhood. Despite his young age, Price was well known to police because he had been committing burglaries and using drugs for years. Price was also reportedly a Peeping Tom, a behavior sexual predators often engage in before moving on to more serious crimes.

Price reportedly lied to detectives about a cut on his hand. After Price failed a lie detector test, detectives decided to search his family home. Surprisingly, they found a large amount of evidence in a shed behind the house, including bloody knives stolen from the Heaton home, bloody clothing, and bloody gloves. Price was arrested and taken to the local station house, where he eventually confessed to the Heaton murders.

Botched Burglary or Premeditated Murder

Price admitted that he broke into the Heaton house with the intention of robbing it. He claimed that he didn't know that anybody was inside until he encountered the residents. Price then admitted the violent nature of the crime; he admitted biting one of the girls in the face and hitting Melissa over the head with a stool.

The testimony made Price sound fairly inept. He claimed he didn't realize he had left a trail of bloody footprints and he accidently stabbed himself during the attack. The forensic examination of the crime scene lent credence to Price's story.

After the Heaton confession, the detectives asked Price about the Spencer murder. To their surprise and disgust, Craig admitted that he had killed Rebecca Spencer as well.

A Sentence of Just Five Years in Reform School

The most outrageous aspect of the crime was the sentence that Craig Price eventually received. On Sept. 21, 1989, Judge Carmine R. DiPetrillo sentenced Price to just five years in jail, even though he had confessed to four brutal murders.

Instead of prison, Price was sent to the Youth Correctional Center at the Rhode Island Training School. In other words, Craig Price would only serve five years in reform school for four brutal murders. He was also ordered to undergo psychological therapy while at the school.

Craig Price did learn one thing while he was at reform school; how to work the system to escape punishment. He refused to go along with the psychological treatment because of the Fifth Amendment to the U.S. Constitution, which bans self-incrimination. Despite his lack of cooperation, Price was labeled a model student and reportedly counseled other students. A 1993 article in The Providence Journal newspaper indicates that Price may have served as a security guard at the school.

The People vs. Craig Price

Not surprisingly, Rhode Island residents became outraged when the press reported on Price's lenient treatment and impending release. Marie and Mary Lou Bouchard were among those leading the efforts to block his release. Their efforts were successful; the Rhode Island state legislature passed a measure called the O'Neil bill designed to give the state Attorney General's office the right to keep mentally ill teenagers institutionalized indefinitely.

As it turned out, the laws and other efforts, such as a demonstration at a visit by then President Bill Clinton, proved unnecessary. In June 1994, Price was indicted for assault and extortion because of threats he had made against a correctional officer. A legal technicality then blocked Price's hopes of release.

A Technicality kept him Behind Bars

Many child killers avoid punishment because of a legal technicality. It was such a technicality that kept Price incarcerated. He had refused to comply with Judge DiPetrillo's order to undergone a psychiatric evaluation. That meant Price was technically in contempt of court.

A team of psychiatrists examined Price and determined that he had lied about the murders. The evaluation was followed by a trial for assault on Oct. 3, 1994. Price was convicted of extortion and simple assault three days later. Incredibly, this time he was sentenced to 15 years to be served in a prison for adults. Eight years of the 15-year sentence were suspended.

The absurdity of the situation was obvious; Price couldn't be imprisoned for four murders, but he could be sentenced to years in prison for threatening a corrections officer. Once in the pen, Price got into more trouble; he was convicted of assault again and sentenced to another in jail after biting a corrections officer's finger in 1996.

Still in Prison for Crimes Committed Behind Bars

Craig Price is still in prison for crimes committed behind bars in 1996; he was sentenced to another 25 years in prison for contempt of court. Seven more years were added to that sentence for assaulting a corrections officer. In 2001, Price was sentenced to four more years for another assault on a guard.

News reports indicate that the earliest possible release date for Craig Price is February 2022. Price is currently serving his sentence in Florida because of overcrowding in Rhode Island prisons. The latest media reports indicate that he is acting as his own attorney and appealing the sentence. Price has been demanding a return to Rhode Island to appear before the state's Supreme Court.

Price is now claiming that he is the victim of racism because he is African-American. He also claims he has paid his debt to society, but nobody in Rhode Island seems to believe either claim.

Bibliography

Bell, Rachel. "Craig Price: Confessions of a Teenage Serial Killer ." n.d. trutv.com/library/crime . Online Encyclopedia Entry . 13 February 2013.

Crime Life . "Craig Price ." n.d. crime-life.com/killers/price . Online Encyclopedia Entry . 13 February 2013.

Wikipedia . "Craig Price ." n.d. en.wikipedia.org . Online Encyclopedia Entry . 13 February 2013.

Wikipedia. "Richard Ramirez." n.d. en.wikipedia.org. Online Encyclopedia Entry. 24 January 2013.

WPRI Staff . "Notorious killer wants to return to RI." 10 February 2011. wpri.com . Online News Article . 13 February 2013.

ERIC SMITH: 13-YEAR-OLD MURDERER AND SEXUAL PREDATOR

Introduction

Eric Smith was among the most notorious child killers in American history. Even though the 13-year-old looked far younger than his age, his crime was horrendous enough to earn a sentence of life in prison.

In fact, Smith's murder and sexual assault of a four-year-old was so barbaric and brutal it fueled agitation for a change in the law. The victim's family and the public were so outraged they demanded that the State change the law so killers like Smith could face a sentence of first degree murder. At the time of the killing, Smith could only be sentenced to second degree murder because of New York state law.

The Murderous Child Molester who looked Like a Child Himself

The abduction, sexual assault, and murder of a child is one of every parent's worst nightmares. Most parents live in fear of strangers that perpetuate such outrages and warn their children about strange adults. Few of them ever warn their children about the danger posed by other kids because they don't imagine the murderous sexual predator to be a 13-year-old boy on a bicycle.

Yet that was exactly who murdered, abused, and mutilated four-year-old Derrick Robie in Savona, New York, on August 2, 1993—a 13-year old boy. The boy was Eric Smith, and he lured Robie away to his death.

A Brutal Crime

The murder of Derrick Robie was particularly horrific and outrageous. According to court documents, Smith choked and strangled Robie. After that, he apparently dropped two large rocks on the boy's head to kill him. He then sodomized the boy's body with a tree limb and mutilated it.

Ironically enough, Smith and Robie were heading to the same location at the time of the murder—a summer day camp for kids. Robie was walking from his home to the camp, and Smith was riding a bicycle. To make matters worse, the scene of the murder—a patch of woods—was only a short distance from Robie's home.

Searchers started looking for Robie once he didn't arrive at summer camp. They discovered the boy's body in the woods, where Smith had dumped it earlier in the day.

The brutal crime would tear apart the small village of Savona, where both boys lived and apparently knew each other. The village was rocked by fear for three days until Smith finally confessed to the crime. The anger at Smith continues to this day.

The Murderer Who Looked Like a Boy

The murder was made particularly horrific by the fact that Smith looked far younger than his 13 years at the time. Pictures show him to be a pudgy boy with red hair and glasses, who looked to be about ten years old.

Despite his youthful appearance, prosecutors decided to try Eric Smith as an adult. The sheer violence and horror of his crime apparently justified that decision. Part of the reason why the crime was so horrific was that both boys had been attending the same day camp together all summer.

The trial that followed deepened the divisions in the community. Defense attorneys tried to prove that Eric was mentally ill and called a psychiatrist, who attested that Smith suffered from intermittent explosive disorder. That disorder causes people to unexpectedly explode in rage and violence, much like Dr. Jekyll's transformation into the beastly Mr. Hyde. Other testimony showed that Smith had been savagely teased by bullies at school and in the community because of his boyish appearance.

The testimony failed, and Smith was convicted of second degree murder and given a sentence of nine years to life in state prison. In a development that angered many people, a technicality in New York state law made Smith eligible for parole in just nine years, in 2002.

Anger at Smith Rages to This Day

The anger at Eric Smith has never abated, and it flairs up again every time he is eligible for parole. Since Smith comes up for parole every two years, the fury never seems to die. Smith served six years in a juvenile facility before he was sent to state prison in Dannemora, New York.

Smith was first eligible for parole in 2002 and has had at least five more parole hearings since then, the last being in April 2012. At the last hearing, the Board ruled that Smith had shown no remorse for his senseless and violent acts, so he wasn't eligible for parole. Smith has been turned down for parole every time he has applied. Recent news articles indicate that he might be released in 2014 after his next parole hearing.

Smith's killing and the subsequent murder of Penny Brown by a 15-year-old in 1999 prompted the New York state legislature to pass Penny's Law. Penny's Law gives courts the power to sentence under-aged murderers such as Eric Smith to 15 to 25 years to life in prison.

The Fight Continues

Every time Eric Smith comes up for parole, Derrick Robie's parents testify against him at the parole board. They often take their case to the media as well as demanding that no leniency be allowed for such under-aged killers.

Eric Smith remains in prison in Dannemora, where he occasionally grants interviews to the press. Smith has promised the parole board and reporters that he will never return to Savona. Recent photographs show that Smith is still baby–faced, but he has tried to make himself appear older by shaving his head and growing a beard and mustache. He has told the parole board that he would like to work as an electrician if he is ever released.

Derrick Robie is still well remembered; media reports indicate that a Facebook page set up in his memory has 3,000 friends. Derrick is also memorialized on several pages on the Internet.

Bibliography

Mauro, Marisa. "Children Who Murder: Jordan Brown, Eric Smith and Others." 13 February 2010. psychologytoday.com. Psychology Today Blog. 11 February 2013.

Penny's Law. "Derrick Robie." 3 January 2009. pennyslaw.com. Online memorial to Derrick Robie. 11 February 2013.

Walsh, Patrice. "Fighting for Derrick." 15 May 2012. www.13wham.com. Online News Article. 11 February 2013.

Wikipedia. "Eric Smith." n.d. en.wikipedia.com. Online Encyclopedia Entry. 11 February 2013.

Zick, John. "Eric Smith denied parole again." 9 April 2010. www.the-leader.com. Corning Leader Newspaper Article. 11 February 2013.

—. "Smith: I wouldn't return to Savona." 4 June 2012. steubencourier.com/news. Steuben Courier Newspaper Article. 11 February 2013.

GEORGE STINNEY JR.: THE YOUNGEST PERSON EVER SENT TO THE ELECTRIC CHAIR

Introduction

Child killers often provoke controversy, particularly when they expose racial and political fault lines in a society. One alleged American child killer, George Junius Stinney Jr., has become a symbol in the modern American debate over the death penalty. Stinney is also used as a symbol of the racism and injustice that was rampant in the United States in the mid-20th century. People are still working to clear Stinney's name and get him a pardon, even though he was executed almost 70 years ago. Like many suspects in brutal murders, George Stinney has become something of a celebrity because of the publicity his case has been attracting since World War II.

The Youngest Person Electrocuted

At the age of 14, George Junius Stinney Jr. was the youngest person ever executed in the electric chair in the United States. He was also the youngest person executed in the 20th century in the United States and the youngest individual ever sentenced to death in America.

His case still provokes controversy, even though he died nearly 70 years ago. The reason for the controversy is obvious: some people who have examined his case believe that Stinney was probably innocent.

Stinney was either a monster and a would-be serial killer or the victim of racism and a politically motivated prosecution. The crime he was accused of was pretty heinous; he beat two young girls to death with a railroad spike. Yet many people believe Stinney was innocent because he was a young African-American man tried in the South at the height of segregation.

Savage Murder with a Railroad Spike

The crime began innocently on March 22, 1944 during the height of World War II. The battlefields were far away from the small town of Alcolu, S.C., but different kinds of evil lurked in the community. On that day, two young girls, eight-year-old Mary Emma Thames and Betty June Binnicker, went out for a bicycle ride.

During the ride, the girls, who were white, stopped to ask 14-year-old George Stinney, who was black, where they could find some wild flowers. They were never seen alive again. When the girls didn't come home, search parties were organized, and Stinney, like most people in the community, joined in.

The next morning, the girls' bodies were found in a ditch. They had been beaten to death with a heavy railroad spike. At the time, the media didn't say whether the girls had been sexually assaulted or not. American news outlets didn't start reporting details of such crimes until decades later.

Was he a Victim or a Monster?

George Stinney was arrested shortly after the bodies were discovered, and that's when controversy began. Stinney was arrested because he had been seen in the area and helped in the search.

Stinney's behavior during the investigation points to his guilt, or at least his involvement in the crime. He confessed to the murders and may have led a sheriff's deputy to the murder weapon, a 14-inch long railroad spike. Spinney even gave a plausible motive for the crime; he said he wanted to have sex with Betty June, but she turned him down.

Stinney's case does have some similarity to other child murderers. Robert Thompson, who killed a four-year-old boy in Liverpool, England in 1993, brought flowers to a memorial for his victim. Craig Price broke into a home and stabbed a woman to death when he was just 13 years old.

Doubts about Stinney's Guilt and Racism

Not surprisingly, racism quickly reared its ugly head in the case. Shortly after Stinney's arrest, a lynch mob formed and moved on the jail where he was held. Deputies saved Stinney from being lynched by moving him to Columbia, S.C.

Stinney went on trial just a month later in Manning, S.C. The trial itself was very questionable because the defense attorney, Charles Plowden, called no witnesses and made no effort to cross-examine the prosecution's witnesses. Instead, Plowden simply argued that

Stinney was too young to be executed, which was apparently not valid under South Carolina state law.

Plowden might have been motivated by politics; he wanted to run for office and he knew that a successful defense could cost him votes. The attorney might also been afraid of a lynch mob or the Ku Klux Klan. Some observers also note that Plowden had little experience in criminal law at the time of the Stinney trial.

Stinney was convicted after the jury deliberated for just five minutes. He was then sentenced to die in the electric chair.

Controversy Erupts

Despite its sensational nature, the Stinney case wasn't well-reported because the media was focusing on World War II. It wasn't until stories started appearing in the African American press in Mid-June shortly before the scheduled execution that the case generated controversy and attracted attention. A number of organizations, including the African American Episcopal (AME) Church and the NAACP, began petitioning South Carolina Governor Olin D. Johnston to pardon Stinney so he could avoid execution.

There is little indication that the opponents thought Stinney was innocent in 1944. Instead, the argument was that executing a child would make America look bad in the eyes of the world. Some critics compared the execution to Hitler and the Nazis.

Johnston ignored the pleas and the execution went forward on June 16, 1944. It took 2,400-volt jolts to kill the 5-foot-1, 95-pound Stinney. The case then largely disappeared into history, although it has occasionally been raised by death penalty opponents and civil rights activists.

Was Stinney Guilty or the Victim of White Racism?

Some modern observers believe that George Stinney's innocence can be proven by examining the record of the case. They note that Stinney might have been too small to pick up the murder weapon, which weighed 14 pounds. That argument seems doubtful; it is fairly easy for a 95-pound person to lift such an object.

An activist and former Alcou resident named George Frierson claims that a member of a prominent local white family committed the murders. He also claims a relative of that person served on a grand jury that investigated the case and recommended Stinney's execution. Frierson did not present any evidence to verify his claims, nor did he name the prominent white suspect.

Questionable Investigation

It is obvious that neither the investigation nor the trial met modern standards, although they were fairly typical of rural American justice in 1944. Stinney does appear to have been railroaded and not given a proper trial, yet the critics have not proved his innocence either.

After nearly 70 years, it is probably impossible to prove George Stinney's guilt or innocence. The physical evidence is long gone, and so is much of the written evidence, which includes the transcript of the trial. Most of the witnesses are probably long dead.

This lack of evidence isn't stopping Frierson and an attorney named Steve McKenzie, who

are campaigning to get Stinney pardoned. One
thing is certain: a pardon today will not do
George Stinney Jr. any good.

Bibliography

Edwards, David. "New evidence could clear 14-year-old executed by South Carolina ." 3 October 2011. rawstory.com . News Article . 14 February 2013.

Gado, Mark. "George Junius Stinney Jr." n.d. muderpedia.org. True Crime Blog Spot Story Posted at Murderpedia. 14 February 2013.

Murderpedia . "George Junius Stinney Jr. ." n.d. murderpedia.org . Online Encyclopedia Entry . 14 February 2013.

Scott, Shirley Lynn. "Death of James Bulger
." n.d. trutv.com/library/crime. Online Encyclopedia Entry . 12 February 2013.

Starr, Terrell Jermaine. "Executed at 14:
George Stinney's Birthday Reminds Us that the
Death Penality Must End ." 19 October 2012.
newsone.com . Editorial . 13 February 2013.

Wikipedia . "Craig Price ." n.d.
en.wikipedia.org . Online Encyclopedia Entry .
13 February 2013.

GRAHAM YOUNG:

TEENAGED MAD SCIENTIST

AND POISONER

Introduction

Psychopaths are among the most dangerous

individuals because they can easily disguise

themselves as normal people. Brilliant psycho-

paths can even figure out how to fool psychologists, psychiatrists, and other experts into
thinking they are normal. Psychopathic child
killers usually learn how to work the system and
fool authority figures early on in life. A typical
example was the teenaged London poisoner
Graham Young, who managed to convince the
chief psychologist at Britain's top mental hospital that he was reformed. The psychologist released Young, even though he had killed his
own stepmother with poison and tried to poison his father, sister, and uncle. Once released,
Young started poisoning again and eventually
killed two coworkers. The Young case proves
how easy it is for psychopaths to manipulate
the system and how dangerous they really are.

The Teenaged Poisoner

Englishman Graham Young is unique in the annals of teenaged murder for one reason: his weapon of choice, poison, is a rare weapon and almost never used by young killers. Yet Young developed an affinity for it that eventually became his undoing.

Young was also one of the scariest young serial killers because he tried to poison almost everybody around him, including friends, coworkers, and members of his own family. The poisoning was done as an experiment to see its effects. He eventually succeeded in killing his own stepmother with the poison and tried to poison his father and sister.

The Boy Who Loved Poison

Growing up in North London in the 1950s and 1960s, Graham Young had two unusual interests for a young Englishman. The first was poison: his hobby was making poison and other dangerous liquids with his chemistry set. The other was Nazism: Young openly admired Hitler and other Nazi leaders and often voiced his admiration for them, something that didn't win him many friends in a city that had been bombed by the Nazis just 20 years before.

Graham was an intelligent boy that liked to experiment. Unfortunately, his experiments showed the work of an evil mind; he made bombs, flammable liquids, and poisons. To see if the poisons worked, Graham started giving them to his classmates at school. Frighteningly enough, by the time he was 17, Graham had accumulated enough poison to kill 300 people.

He used it in other ways; when his friend, Christopher Williams, scheduled a date with a girl Graham liked, Williams conveniently got sick. That enabled Graham to take the girl out instead. Fortunately for the other kids at Graham's school, he decided to start poisoning his own family.

Poisoning his Own Family

Graham Young's most horrendous experiment was to poison his own family, including his stepmother, Molly Young. She died in 1962, but Graham was never suspected because he talked his dad into cremating his stepmother's body. The family thought Molly had died of complications from an accident. Instead, Graham had poisoned her with a colorless and tasteless heavy metal, thallium.

Other members of the family were next, including Graham's Uncle John, who got sick at Molly's funeral. Graham had apparently put poisoned pickles out for family members to try. Uncle John recovered, and the next victim was Graham's father Fred. Graham started slipping toxins into Fred's beer while he was at the local pub.

Some people think that Fred Young may have suspected Graham, but failed to turn the 14-year-old into the authorities. Instead, it was Graham's chemistry teacher, Geoffrey Hughes, who alerted the police. The police arranged an interview between Graham and a career expert (in reality, a police psychologist). The psychologist talked Graham into telling him about his "hobby." The interview led police to uncover several stashes of poison Graham had stored around his home.

Sent to a Maximum Security Mental Hospital

Graham Young was eventually convicted of poisoning his father, his sister, and Chris Williams. The court sent Graham to Broadmoor, a maximum security mental hospital, and recommended that he not be released without the permission of Britain's home secretary.

The stay at Broadmoor made Graham worse, not better; he became a more devoted Nazi and may have even figured out how to poison another prisoner, John Berridge, with cyanide in the hospital. Eventually, Graham Young pretended to conform and convinced psychologists that he was a model prisoner.

The problem was that Young wasn't cured at all, he was simply manipulating authorities to win his release. Fellow inmates who actually had to live with Young thought he was as violent and dangerous as ever. He may have kept up his activities in 1968; toxic soap was discovered in a tea maker at Broadmoor. Nobody knows who put it there, but enough poison had been added to the tea to burn the stomachs of 97 people. Fortunately, nobody drank the tea, but Young would soon have more chances to give victims poisoned tea.

Release and a Return to Poisoning

In 1970, prison psychologist Dr. Edgar Udwin recommended that Graham Young be released. Udwin claimed Young was no longer obsessed with poison and violence. In reality, Young was simply lying to Udwin. A nurse who worked closely with Young heard a different story: Young said he planned to kill one person for every year he had spent at Broadmoor.

Graham Young walked free in February 1971 and returned to North London. Once he got home, he didn't seem changed at all; he still voiced his admiration of Hitler and talked about a final solution. Young also visited his old neighborhood, Neasden, and began telling former neighbors he was back.

Young started poisoning again within a week of his release. Shortly after Young moved into a youth hostel, a fellow resident, Trevor Sparkes, began experiencing mysterious cramps, pains, and diarrhea. Doctors couldn't find a cause for Sparkes's problems, but if they had checked for poison, they would have.

Sparkes survived, but another man may have died because of Young at the time. The man reportedly committed suicide because he

couldn't stand the intense pain. The pain started after the man drank a beer with a young
man that sounded like Graham Young. The man
was obsessed with poisons.

Mysterious Illness in the Workplace

Using a letter of recommendation from the
ever gullible Dr. Udwin, Graham Young got a
job at a photo processing company, John Hadland Ltd. The company employed toxic chemicals in its photo processing, and Young's job
involved working with those substances.

Shortly after Young started working at John
Hadland, employees started coming down with
a mysterious illness, just like his family members had. Many of them developed diarrhea
and stomach pains after Graham Young politely
fetched them a cup of tea. On July 7, 1971,
one of Young's coworkers, Bob Egle, died; the

cause of death was listed as pneumonia probably caused by burns to his throat from the acid
in Graham Young's tea. Young showed his con-
cern and even went to Egle's funeral.

The mysterious ailments were blamed on a
virus, probably because the John Hadland employees and their doctors didn't realize Graham Young's true identity or his past. Only
when police were called in after another death
did Young fall under suspicion.

The Teacup Poisoner admits all

Police arrested Graham Young on Nov. 21,
1971, and he quickly admitted everything. He
even bragged about committing the perfect
murder, the killing of his stepmother.

When he was tried for murder, Young told
the court he was proud to be the first person
to use thallium in a poisoning case in Great

Britain. The boastfulness didn't help Young: he was convicted of two murders, two attempted murders, and two counts of administering poison. Young's manner frightened jurors, who became horrified when they learned that he had poisoned before and been released from a maximum security mental institution just months earlier.

The press labeled Graham Young "the Teacup Poisoner" and "the St. Alban's Poisoner." He was sentenced to four terms of life imprisonment without parole. Young was sent to Parkhurst, Britain's toughest maximum security prison; there, his fellow inmates included the Moors Murderer, Ian Brady, whom he played chess with.

Immortalized in Wax

Graham Young died in Parkhurst in 1990; the cause of death was listed as a heart attack, but many suspect Young poisoned himself or was murdered by another inmate. After his death, one of Graham Young's boyhood wishes came true. A wax version of Young is now housed at Madame Tussaud's wax museum in London, where impressions of famous murderers are on display. Young's impression is in the Chamber of Horrors with Dr. Crippin, a Victorian poisoner whom Graham admired as a young man.

Bibliography

Murder UK. "Graham Young ." n.d. murderuk.org. Online Encyclopedia Entry . 16 February 2013.

Sharp, Johnny. "Graham Young, the St. Albans Poisoner ." n.d. trutv.com/library . Online Encyclopedia Entry. 16 February 2013.

Wikipedia . "Graham Young ." n.d. en.wikipedia.org. Online Encyclopedia Entry . 16 February 2013.

JESSE POMEROY: THE BOY FIEND AND THE YOUNG DEMON

Introduction

Child killers becoming celebrities because of media coverage is nothing new. The first such killer to become a national celebrity in America was Jesse Pomeroy, who terrorized Boston in

1874. Pomeroy had a number of distinctions. He was one of the most sadistic child killers ever. He was also one of the youngest people ever to be sentenced to death in the United States, yet he managed to escape hanging and live for another 56 years. He also spent 41 years in solitary confinement. Even though he was isolated, Pomeroy enjoyed constant media attention because of the nature of his crimes; the torture and murder of two children.

The Boy Fiend

Long before the terms "serial killer" and "sexual predator" were invented, such a monster stalked the streets of Boston. Shockingly, the monster was only 14 years old, yet he was guilty of at least several murders. Pomeroy's crimes were so disturbing that the press labeled him "The Boy Fiend", "The Boy Murderer", "The Child Murderer", and "The Young Demon".

Pomeroy was a ruthless and sadistic killer who tied up and tortured his victims, then mutilated their bodies. Like many serial killers and child murderers, he was well known to the police before his killing spree. He had been arrested and released to his mother's custody before the crimes.

The First Child Serial Killer in American History

Jesse Pomeroy set many firsts. He was the first child killer to make national headlines in 1874 and the first famous serial killer in American history. He was also one of the most brutal and sadistic killer kids in history.

Pomeroy came from a respectable working class family in the Boston area. His mother was a dressmaker and his father worked in a market. There was little to indicate that he was a monster or what caused his crimes, yet he apparently got started on torture and violence when he was 12 years old.

In 1871 and 1872, Jesse, then only 12 or 13, lured several boys to a remote area in Chelsea, Mass. where he was living. Once he got them alone, Pomeroy savagely tortured his would-be victims.

The New York Times reported that he stripped a boy naked, tied him to a telegraph pole, whipped him, and cut him with a knife in the head. Another newspaper report indicated that he stripped another boy naked in below zero temperatures, mutilated him with a knife, and left him alone.

Imprisoned and Released to his Mother's Custody

Jesse Pomeroy's behavior was so bad that he was eventually arrested and sentenced to a boys' reform school for six years. Incredibly, he only served one year and five months and was released for good behavior. Like many psychopaths, Pomeroy knew how and when to behave himself to game the system in his favor. Once out, he went to live with his family in their new home in South Boston.

Pomeroy wasn't reformed at all; as soon as he was released, he began raising the level of his violence. On April 23, 1871, Pomeroy stabbed four-year-old Horace Moran several times, mutilated his body, and dumped it in a marsh. Police investigated and quickly turned their attention to Pomeroy. The police were aware of Pomeroy's record and figured he was a logical suspect.

Detectives took plaster casts of footprints found near the boy's body. They also matched mud on Pomeroy's boots to the mud in Dorchester Marsh where the body had been dumped.

Another Murder and a Criminal who was Too Young to Hang

Jesse Pomeroy eventually confessed to two murders, that of the boy and one the police didn't know about. Pomeroy had also cut the throat of a 10-year-old girl he had lured into the basement of his mother's dressmaking shop. The body of the girl, Katie Curran, was found under an ash heap in the basement.

Jesse Pomeroy became one of the youngest people sentenced to death in American history in December, 1874. His trial was considered so important that the state's attorney general himself prosecuted Pomeroy. The jury sentenced Pomeroy to hang for the two murders, but Massachusetts Governor William Gaston couldn't bring himself to sign the execution order or death warrant.

Over the next year and a half, prosecutors and the state's Governor's Council kept pushing for the death penalty, but Gaston resisted. Gaston felt that Pomeroy was simply too young to be executed. Eventually, the situation was resolved when the Council voted to commute Pomeroy's sentence to life imprisonment.

The First Media Sensation Serial Killer

Jesse Pomeroy became one of the first killers to become a celebrity in the United States because of the time he lived. Mass-circulation daily newspapers were just becoming popular, and they needed something to report on. Then, as now, stories about sensational murders sold newspapers.

Pomeroy's activities and the media circus surrounding them made perfect copy for the yellow journalists to write about. He became such a national figure that he was still the subject of a great deal of media attention years later, even though he was held in solitary confinement for many years. The Boston Globe often carried stories about Pomeroy's activities in the state prison in Charlestown, Mass.

In Prison for Over Half a Century

Jesse Pomeroy spent 56 years in prison and 41 years in solitary confinement. During his time in jail, Pomeroy demonstrated his intelligence; he learned several foreign languages, including German and Arabic, read law books, and drafted legal challenges to his sentences. Pomeroy even wrote poetry and tried to get it published.

He also made between 10 and 12 escape attempts. On several occasions, prison officials found homemade tools, including drills, in Pomeroy's cell. Another time, Pomeroy caused a gas pipe to explode in an escape attempt. He didn't escape, but he lost an eye in the attempt.

Pomeroy was let out of solitary in 1917, but he never left custody. Instead, he died in the Bridgewater Hospital for the Criminally Insane on Sept. 30, 1932. He had been transferred there in 1929 because of his frail health. Jesse Pomeroy managed to cheat death, but never regained his freedom.

Bibliography

Celebrate Boston . "Jesse Pomeroy The Boy Fiend ." n.d. celebrateboston.com. Boston History Article . 16 February 2013.

Wikipedia. "Jesse Pomeory." n.d. en.wikipedia.org. Online Encyclopedia Entry . 16 February 2013.

JOSHUA PHILLIPS: THE 14-YEAR-OLD KILLER NEXT DOOR

Introduction

Murder cases involving young suspects often take very bizarre turns. One of the strangest is that of 14-year-old Joshua Phillips, who stabbed, strangled, and beat a little girl to death, then hid her body under his bed for a week. The case is made even stranger by Joshua's claims that he accidently killed 8-year-old Maddie Clifton during a baseball game. Even though the murder occurred in 1998, Phillips' case is not going away anytime soon. In another strange twist, a recent U.S. Supreme Court decision has brought the bizarre affair back into the headlines. Some child-killer cases never seem to go away.

Looking in all the Wrong Places

When 8-year-old Maddie Clifton vanished from her neighborhood in Jacksonville, Fla. in November 1998, nobody suspected that her body was under the bed of a 14-year-old boy. The boy's name was Joshua Phillips and he had no history of violence, yet a little girl's body was hidden under his bed for a week.

Police and others had been searching everywhere, including dumpsters and nearby woods. Nobody thought to look under Joshua's bed or consider him a suspect. Instead, cops investigated another neighbor who had been investigated for sex crimes in the past. Joshua didn't even appear on their radar, even though he was the killer.

Authorities, including the FBI, were baffled by the case. Search parties that included 400 volunteers were sent out. Chillingly, one of the volunteers was Joshua Phillips, the actual murderer, yet nobody connected him to the case.

The Dead Little Girl under the Bed

Maddie's body wasn't discovered by the police or search parties; it was discovered a week later by Josh's mother, Melissa Phillips. Melissa went into Josh's room because she thought a waterbed was leaking. Instead, she discovered the little girl's body. The mother immediately ran from the house and came back with the police.

Incredibly, Joshua had been acting normally in the week since the murder. He returned to school and acted like just another teenaged boy. That changed when police took him out of class and placed him under arrest.

Joshua then told the police a story that nobody seemed to believe. Incredible as it was, he claimed the girl's death was an accident, although it's hard to believe those claims because of the brutality of the crime.

Did a Baseball Cause a Little Girl's Death?

Joshua claimed that he had hit Maddie in the head with a baseball, which caused her to collapse. Instead of seeking help, he carried her to his room, and she began to cry. Fearing that his dad would punish him, Joshua admitted to trying to silence Maddie by hitting her with a baseball bat and stabbing her. He then shoved her body under the bed to cover up the crime.

Phillips' story sounds incredible; a normal 14-year-old would have called for help. A more likely scenario is that Joshua lured Maddie to his room and killed her. What he did the next week was particularly disturbing. He simply forgot about the body and ignored it for a week. Those who examined Joshua claimed he was living in a fantasy world.

An autopsy revealed that Joshua had stabbed Maddie 11 times and tried to strangle her with a telephone cord. Another version of the story in which Josh hit Maddie in the eye with a baseball bat, then dragged her up to his room, has also come to light.

Was the Crime Sexually Motivated?

The abduction and killing of Maddie Clifton might have been sexually motivated. Police reportedly found violent pornography in Joshua's possession. The nature of the pornography has never been divulged to the public.

No evidence that Maddie Clifton was actually assaulted has ever come to light. One possibility is that Josh tried to assault her and ended up killing her in the process.

A Mother's Battle for her Son

In a controversial move, Joshua Phillips was charged and tried as an adult. That enabled prosecutors to file first-degree murder charges against him. Even though he was charged as an adult, Phillips could not receive the death penalty under Florida law because the crime was committed when he was 14.

Phillips was convicted of first-degree murder in August 1999, and he was sentenced to life in prison without parole. Since then, his mother has been fighting to have his sentenced reduced to second-degree murder. If Phillips' charges are reduced, he might one day be eligible for parole.

Melissa Phillips has done numerous media interviews in her efforts to free her son. In her talks with the media, Melissa admits that her son is guilty, but seems to believe the accident story. Incredibly, Melissa remains on friendly terms with Sheila DeLongis, Maddie Clifton's mother.

The fight over Joshua Phillips continues in cyberspace, where a website devoted to freeing Josh and a website honoring Maddie exist. It is unclear if Sheila DeLongis and Maddie Clifton are connected with these websites or not.

The Supreme Court Might set him Free

Joshua Phillips is still serving his sentence in the Florida state prison system, but a 2012 ruling in a case called Miller v. Alabama might give him a chance at freedom. In that case, the court ruled that it is unconstitutional to sentence juveniles to life in prison without parole.

Phillips' attorney, Tom Fallis, told the press that he thinks the case will enable him to appeal his client's sentence. If the appeal is successful, it is unclear if Phillips will get released. Even he is eligible for parole, Phillips would still need a parole board's approval to get out. It is doubtful that the state's parole board will ever release him.

Interestingly enough, the prosecutor who won the life sentence against Joshua Phillips now regrets it. Harry Shorstein, a former state attorney, told the media that he now thinks it was wrong to sentence a teenager to life in prison without parole. Shorstein has changed his mind because he thinks that recent scientific discoveries prove that teenagers' brains are not fully developed, so they are less responsible for their actions. Whether the courts will ever buy this argument or not remains to be seen.

Bibliography

CBS News . "Why Did Josh Kill?" 11 February 2011. cbsnews.com. 48 Hours Story . 15 February 2013.

Jacksonville Criminal Defense . "Free Josh ." n.d. freejosh.com . Website Defending Josh Phillips . 15 February 2013.

Leung, Rebecca. "Caged Kids Life Sentence ." 5 December 2007. cbsnews.com. Interview with Melissa Phillips . 15 February 2013.

Maddie Clifton Memorial Fund. "MaddieClifton.org." n.d. maddieclifton.org . Online Memorial to Maddie Clifton. 15 February 2013.

Monacelli, Antonia. "Murderous Children: 14-Year Old Joshua Philllips Murdered His 8 Year Old Neighbor." n.d. antonia-monacelli.hubpages.com . Online Profile . 15 Febraury 2013.

News 4 Jacksonville Staff . "Mother of Convicted Killer Wants New Trial for Son ." 14 October 2011. news4jax.com. News Article . 15 February 2013.

Schoettler, Jim. "Supreme Court ruling on juveniles to impact high-profile Jacksonville murder cases ." 25 June 2012. jacksonville.com . News Article . 15 February 2013.

Supreme Court of the United States . "Syllabus Miller v. Alabama ." October 2011. supremecourt.gov/opinions/2011. PDF of

Syllabus of Appeal to US Supreme Court . 15 February 2013.

Wikipedia. "Josh Phillips (murderer)." n.d. en.wikipedia.org. Online Encyclopedia Entry. 14 February 2013.

MARY BELL: CHILD KILLER AND TABLOID SENSATION

Introduction

Most child killers fade into obscurity as they grow up. One—Britain's Mary Bell—seems to have attracted more attention after she grew up and got out of prison than when she committed her actual crime. That's quite a feat because Bell's crime was especially noteworthy and heinous: she brutally murdered two little boys.

Ms. Bell again became a tabloid sensation 30 years after the actual crime. She attracted so much attention that she required police protection and eventually had to apply to the courts for the right to live in anonymity. Even though she was a vicious psychopath, Mary Bell was no match for Britain's rabid tabloid journalists.

She Killed Two Little Boys

Mary Bell is one of the most unusual serial killers in the history of crime. Her life story is a bizarre one because she went from serial killer to tabloid sensation to loving mother. The young girl presented a serious challenge to

British society and provided decades of entertainment to tabloid readers.

Mary Bell has been described as both a loving mother and as intelligent, manipulative, and dangerous. When she was just 11 years old, Mary murdered two young children and tried to kill at least four more. Yet she was later described as a loving mother of a daughter living a normal, English working-class existence.

A Horrendous Childhood

Mary Bell's childhood was definitely a nightmare; her mother Betty Bell was both mentally ill and a prostitute. Mary didn't know who her father was but suspected it was Billy Bell, a career criminal who had served time for armed robbery. Some accounts suggest Mary's real father may have been one of Betty's customers.

Growing up in poverty in the dismal British industrial city of Newcastle, Mary faced numerous horrors. She suffered a number of drug overdoses that may have been attempts by her mother to kill her. Betty Bell also once tried to give Mary to a stranger. If that wasn't bad enough, some accounts indicate Betty prostituted Mary to some of her customers.

A Murderous Rampage at Age 11

Mary Bell started her murderous rampage as she approached her 11th birthday in the summer of 1968. Her first victim was a three-year-old boy, a cousin of Mary's, whom she pushed off a ledge on May 11.

The next day, on May 12, Mary attacked three girls who were playing outside. She tried to strangle one of them, and her attack was so violent that the police were called. Mary's friend, Norma Bell (no relation), reportedly told constables that Mary was trying to figure out how to strangle or choke somebody to death. Incredibly, neither of the girls was arrested, and they were allowed to go free. Instead, the girls were "warned about their conduct."

The warning did little good because, ten days later, on May 25, 1968, Mary celebrated her birthday by strangling four-year-old Martin Brown in an abandoned house. Incredibly, the police believed that Martin's death was an accident and didn't investigate. Local residents believed Brown's death was an accident caused by the terrible condition of old buildings in the neighborhood.

Mary and Norma reportedly broke into a nursery school and vandalized it. Mary supposedly left a note that included a confession to

Martin's murder, but that was dismissed as a prank.

A Horrific Crime

Mary's next crime was incredibly horrific; on July 31, 1968, she and Norma took three-year-old Brian Howe to a vacant lot in the neighborhood. There they strangled the boy and left his body. Mary later returned to the lot and carved an N into Brian's body with a razor. She also mutilated the boy's penis with a pair of scissors and cut off some of his hair.

The boy's body was found that night. Incredibly, Mary and Norma even helped Brian's sister Pat search the neighborhood for the missing boy shortly after the murder.

Pat Howe may have been fooled by Mary Bell, but Inspector James Dobson of the Newcastle Police was not. Dobson began to suspect Mary as soon as he saw her watching Brian Howe's funeral procession. Dobson questioned Norma, who admitted that she had seen Mary kill Brian. She also claimed that Mary had shown her Brian's dead body. Mary was soon arrested and confessed to the crime.

A Psychopath or a Victim?

Like a true sociopath, Mary Bell tried to blame Norma Bell for her crimes. Neither police nor prosecutors believed Mary, although both girls were charged with two counts of manslaughter. Norma Bell was later acquitted by a court, but Mary Bell was convicted of manslaughter.

Mary was charged with manslaughter because psychiatrists had diagnosed her with classic signs of psychopathy. The court sentenced Mary to a term of indefinite imprisonment at Her Majesty's pleasure. Ironically enough, prison authorities didn't know what to do with Mary Bell because the British penal system had no provisions for dealing with 11-year-old murderers.

Ironically enough, Mary Bell first ended up in a reform school for boys. Interestingly, she seemed to reform there even as she picked fights with the boys and drove counselors away. Mary was later housed at an open adult prison and a girls' remand home (the equivalent of an American halfway house). She was released in 1980 after serving 12 years.

A Media Circus

Mary Bell became one of the first celebrities to catch the attention of the British tabloids, which covered her intensely. Part of the reason for the attention was that Betty Bell was constantly talking to reporters and giving them writings she claimed belonged to her daughter. Betty's motivation for talking to the press was money; unlike American media outlets, British newspapers regularly pay sources for juicy stories.

Mary Bell was also the subject of a book by Austrian-born journalist Gitta Sereny, a reporter for The Telegraph newspaper. The book, The Case of Mary Bell, was based on interviews of Mary that Gitta made in prison. Mary herself added to the attention by telling the tabloids how she lost her virginity during an escape from prison in 1977.

Life After Prison: Can a Serial Killer Transform?

When she was released from prison in 1980, Mary Bell was granted anonymity, a British legal practice that allowed her to change her identity. Bell lived quietly under an assumed name in an undisclosed location in England for many years. She also had a daughter by an unnamed man.

Mary Bell came back into the spotlight in 1998 when Gitta Sereny published a second book about her, called Cries Unheard. Sereny unleashed a firestorm of controversy when she announced her intentions to share her profits from the book with Mary Bell. The profits included a £40,000 ($62,612 US) payment from the highly respected Times of London for the serialization rights to the book. Her critics included the Home Secretary and Prime Minister Tony Blair.

The publicity surrounding Cries Unheard helped tabloid reporters track Mary Bell down to her home in Southern England. At that time, Mary's 14-year-old daughter learned of her mother's past and true identity for the first time. The daughter apparently didn't realize that her mum was one of Britain's most notorious serial killers. Media attention got so intense that the police took Bell and her daughter into protective custody.

Mary Bell Today

In 2003 a British High Court granted Mary Bell and her daughter the right to live anonymously for the rest of their lives. That means it is illegal for anybody, including the media, to reveal their identities or locations. The ruling was widely criticized by the British press and the victims' families. The lack of a First Amendment gives the British courts a far greater ability to censor the media than their American counterparts.

Mary Bell and her daughter are apparently living somewhere in Great Britain under assumed identities. Even though she's dropped out of sight, Mary Bell still generates controversy in the psychiatric profession. Her case seems to refute the conventional wisdom that psychopaths and sociopaths cannot be reformed. Nobody knows whether Mary Bell has really changed or simply learned how to adapt to society's mores in order to survive and stay out of prison.

Bibliography

Fraser, Lorraine. "How a 'terrified' Mary Bell walked back into the world." 24 June 2001. telegraph.co.uk. Telegrpah Newspaper Article. 12 February 2013.

McCann, Paul. "Newspapers tarnised by Mary Bell coverage." 1 May 1998. www.independent.co.uk. Newspaper Editorial. 12 February 2013.

Murder UK. "Mary Bell Fact File." 2011. www.murderuk.com/child_killers. Online Fact File. 12 February 2013.

Scott, Shirley Lynn. "Mary Bell." 2011. trutv.com/library/crime. Online Encyclopedia Article. 12 February 2013.

The Telegraph. "Mary Bell, a woman still on teh run from herself ." 22 May 2003. tele-graph.co.uk/news. Telegraph Newspaper Article . 12 February 2013.

Wikipedia. "Gitta Sereny." n.d. en.wikipedia.org. Online Encyclopedia Entry. 12 February 2013.

Wikipedia. "Mary Bell." n.d. en.wikipedia.org. Online Encyclopedia Entry. 12 February 2013.

"J.R.": She Helped Kill Her Family

Introduction

The law is often a child killer's best friend;
legal codes in many countries provide a great
deal of protection to young perpetrators. Leg-
islation often makes the identities of juvenile
offenders a secret and limits the sentences

they can receive. These laws are designed to protect children and give delinquents a chance at a normal life when they grow up. Unfortunately, these laws often help "killer kids" get away with heinous acts. The list of youthful killers that walked free after serving short sentences includes Willie Bosket, Mary Bell, Seito Sakakibara, Graham Young, and Canada's "J.R.". Of these murderers, "J.R." just might be the worst because the law gave her a chance for a normal life while leaving her accomplice and former lover to rot in prison for decades.

From Brutal Killer to College Freshman

Among the students at Mount Royal University in Calgary, Alberta, "J.R." has a unique distinction. She spent 10 years in prison for helping murder her parents and younger sister.

The college student was only 12 when she stabbed her little brother and helped her boyfriend slit his throat.

What's more disturbing is that "J.R." may have lured the man who helped her murder her parents. The motive for the murder is equally chilling: "J.R." reportedly helped kill her parents because they wouldn't let her date a 23-year-old man named Jeremy Allen Steinke.

Authorities and defense attorneys have portrayed "J.R." as a victim who didn't understand what she was doing, yet there is evidence that she is a cold-blooded psychopath who orchestrated the massacre of her own family.

From Goth to Murderer

"J.R." was a rebellious girl who lived in the remote Canadian town of Medicine Hat, Alberta. Like many rebellious girls, she was into vampires, death metal, and the Goth culture. She also spent a lot of time online, where she may have made contact with Steinke. He was so immersed in Goth culture that he claimed be a 300-year-old werewolf.

Police think that "J.R." may have falsely claimed to have been older when she went online. Some of her postings indicate that she posed as a 15-year-old. Something that wasn't hidden was "J.R."'s hatred for her parents.

She had been telling friends, including Jeremy, that she wanted to kill her parents for months. "J.R." even sent Jeremy a message that read "I have a plan. It begins with me killing them and ends with me living with you."

Jeremy retorted he wanted "J.R."'s parents to pay with their blood. It isn't clear what he wanted them to pay for, but pay they would. He also wrote "Their throats I want to slit."

The Werewolf and the Little Girl Strike

The self-proclaimed werewolf and the angry little girl made good their threats on April 22, 2006. That night, Jeremy and "J.R." entered the "J.R."'s family home with bloodlust in their eyes and murder in their hearts.

Jeremy stabbed "J.R."'s father, Marc "J.R.", and her mother, Debra, to death while "J.R." watched. The two then went upstairs and discovered "J.R."'s little brother, eight-year-old Jacob. He reportedly pleaded for his life, but "J.R." stabbed him in the stomach. After the stabbing, Jeremy Steinke slit Jacob's throat as "J.R." watched. "J.R." later said she murdered Jacob because she didn't want him growing up without parents.

The most chilling part of the murder was that Jeremy and "J.R." were seen kissing and laughing at a restaurant just a few hours later. After the murder, the two decided to run away and leave the town. They were apparently helped by Kacy Lancaster, a 19-year-old friend of Jeremy's who drove them away in a pickup truck.

She Got Away Because of her Young Age

The bodies of the "J.R."s were not discovered until the next day when a six-year-boy looked through a window and saw the slaughter. Police started investigating and searching for "J.R.", whom they at first believed to be a victim.

The ugly truth came out when the two were arrested about 80 miles away in Leader, Saskatchewan. Once they were in custody, it became apparent that "J.R." was a murderer, rather than a kidnap victim. Unfortunately, she may have gotten away with her crimes because of her age.

A Canadian law called the Youth Criminal Justice Act prevented the Canadian press from publishing "J.R."'s name. The same law prevented courts from sentencing offenders, including murderers, under the age of 14 to more than 10 years in prison.

She Served Just Eight Years

Even though "J.R." was found guilty of three counts of first degree murder, she ended up serving a little over eight years in prison. At the time, "J.R." was the youngest person convicted of multiple counts of first-degree murder in the history of Canada. The sentence included credit for the 18 months "J.R." served and four years in a psychiatric institution.

"J.R." was released from the psychiatric hospital in 2011 and entered 4½ years of something called "conditional supervision in the community." At the time of her release, psychiatrists claimed that she was showing remorse for her crimes. Whether she actually felt remorse or was simply lying to get her release can't be determined. She enrolled in college at Mount Royal around the time of her release and is still attending the school. Calgary news media refused to publish "J.R."'s name, although they could publish Jeremy's name under Canadian law, which they did.

One thing is clear, however, Jeremy Steinke didn't get off so easily. He was sentenced to life imprisonment in 2008. Unlike "J.R.", Steinke faces a long time behind bars in Alberta's provincial prison system; he won't be eligible for parole for 25 years. Steinke could be hit with such a stiff sentence because he was an adult at the time of the murders.

Is She a Remorseful Victim or a Psychopathic Manipulator?

"J.R." is now living under conditional supervision in Calgary, Alberta and attending Mont Royal University. Few details of her life are available because of Canadian law. It is unclear whether she is still in contact with Jeremy Steinke, who proposed marriage to her at their trial.

Jeremy Steinke, who now calls himself Jackson May, is serving his sentence in prison. Whether he still claims to be a werewolf or not is unknown.

It will probably never be known if "J.R." was the victim of a grownup sexual predator or a vicious psychopathic manipulator. The available evidence indicates she was the manipulator and Steinke her pawn. The murders were apparently "J.R."'s idea and she was the one who would benefit. If that's the case, "J.R." got away with it and ruined another person's life in the process.

Bibliography

Elam, Paul. "Murderess "J.R." ." 14 September 2011. avoiceformen.com. Blog Entry. 17 February 2013.

Japan Times . "Kobe killer set free ." 11 March 2004. murderpedia.org. Japan Times Newspaper Article . 17 February 2013.

Monacelli, Anotnia. "Murderous Children: 12 Year Old "J.R." & Her Boyfriend Murderered Her Parents and 8 Year Old Brother." 2012. antonia-monacelli.hubpages.com . Blog Entry . 17 February 2013.

Murder UK. "Graham Young ." n.d. murderuk.org. Online Encyclopedia Entry . 16 February 2013.

Strashok, Mark. "Multiple killer attends MRU." 14 September 2011. 660news.com . Online news article. 17 February 2013.

Wikipedia . "Kobe child murders." n.d. en.wikipedia.org . Online encyclopedia entry. 17 February 2013.

—. " "J.R." family murders." n.d. en.wikipedia.org. Online Encyclopedia Entry. 17 February 2013.

—. "Willie Bosket ." n.d. en.wikipedia.org. Online Encyclopedia Entry. 16 February 2014.

Wikipedia. "Mary Bell." n.d.

en.wikipedia.org . Online Encyclopedia Entry .

12 February 2013.

Seito Sakakibara: Japan's Mysterious Demon Rose

Introduction

The problem of child killers is a worldwide phenomenon that presents a major dilemma for authorities, courts, and society in general.

American, British, and Japanese authorities have all had a difficult time dealing with child killers. A major problem is that the law in most countries traditionally prevents authorities from trying such malefactors as adults. That means they couldn't face the usual punishment for such crimes, usually the death penalty or life imprisonment. This led to a public outrage, particularly in Japan, where the brutal killer Shinichirou Azuma (or Seito Sakakibara) managed to spend only six years in a reformatory for killing and beheading a mentally challenged boy.

The 14-year-old who Terrorized Kobe

The case of Shinichirou Azuma, who used the alias Seito Sakakibara, is one of the most horrific child killings in history. Azuma murdered and mutilated two children and sent frightening letters to the newspapers about it. The rambling letters add mystery to the case, which continues to generate controversy in Japan to this day.

The crimes were particularly horrifying because the suspect arrested was a 14-year-old school boy. His young age poised a dilemma for the Japanese justice system. In Japan, murderers are traditionally sentenced to death, but Azuma was too young for the death penalty under the law.

The most disturbing aspect of the case may have been that Azuma was imitating earlier serial killers. Like many young people, he idolized certain individuals; unfortunately, those he idolized were sadistic serial killers. The imitation of historic monsters increased the media attention to the case and made it all the more confusing.

This is the Beginning of the Game

The terror began on May 27, 1997, when a janitor found the headless body of June Hase, a mentally challenged boy, at the front gate of Tainohata Elementary School in Kobe. The body had been beheaded and mutilated. To add to the sadistic nature of the crime, a note that began with the words "this is the beginning of the game" was found near the body.

It is obvious that the serial killer didn't just want to kill; he wanted to terrorize the city and its people. To compound the hysteria, a letter signed Seito Sakakibara was sent to the newspaper Kobe Shinbun. The letter echoed the note and contained lots of frightening rhetoric. Some of the rhetoric included "It's only when I kill that I am liberated from the constant hatred that I suffer and I am able to attain peace." The press added to the climate of fear by stating the letter had been signed "Demon's Rose."

The letter spread terror by insinuating that there would be more child killings. It also made clear that Sakakibara was targeting the authoritarian Japanese educational system.

The incident was quickly compared to the Zodiac, a serial killer who terrorized Northern California in the late 1960s. Like the Demon Rose, the Zodiac spread terror by sending letters to the newspapers. There were some differences: the Zodiac used a gun and the killer has never been caught or investigated.

The Demon Rose turns out to be Boy A

The horror of the Hase murder was compounded when police arrested a suspect, a 14-year-old junior high school student who was identified as Boy A. Right after the arrest, Boy

A confessed to the murder of a 10-year-old girl, Ayaka Yamashita, on March 16, 1997. He also confessed to assaults on three girls at that same time.

The police also recovered Boy A's diary, and the writings in it were particularly chilling. On March 16, he wrote that the killing of Ayaka Yamashita was a sacred experiment designed to see how fragile human beings were. He also admitted to beating Yamashita to death with a hammer.

Another bizarre reference in the letter is to something called Bamoidōkishin. This is a Buddhist spirit sometimes associated with anti-Semitism and Nazism because it is often depicted with a Swastika on its face. Boy A thanked Bamoidōkishin for helping him get away with the murder. The spirit is regularly featured as a character in Japanese comic books (or manga) and in anime (or Japanese animation).

Similarities to other Serial Killers

Azuma has some disturbing similarities to other "killer kids" such as Graham Young, London's "teacup poisoner" who regarded his killings as experiments. Another similarity to Young was Azuma's imitation of historic serial killers. Young imitated Victorian poisoners that were often celebrated in British popular culture.

There are also parallels to Japanese serial killer Tsutomu Miyazaki, who murdered and mutilated four girls and molested their corpses in 1989. Miyazaki, who was labeled Dracula by the Japanese press, mailed a postcard to the victim of one of his crimes. He also sent the family of another victim the ashes of her bones.

Controversy Begins

The Kobe murders ignited a political controversy in Japan that eventually reached the
nation's parliament (or Diet). One politician
blamed movies and demanded excessive cen-
sorship. Others noted that under the law in Japan, Azuma couldn't be tried as an adult, which
meant he was not eligible for the death penalty.

In another eerie echo of the Graham Young
case, it was announced in 2004 that Azuma (or
Sakakibara) would be released when he turned
21. Critics quickly noted that the announce-
ment might have been a publicity stunt by the
Japanese Ministry of Justice. They claimed the
ministry was really planning to lock Boy A for a
longer period of time to demonstrate it was
tough on child murderers.

Was he Really Guilty or Not?

The controversy is compounded by allegations that Azuma might be innocent of at least one of the crimes. These allegations are fueled by the secretive nature of the Japanese police and justice system.

Circumstantial evidence seems to lend some support to these allegations. Critics of the investigation have noted that evidence indicates one of the murders was committed by a left-handed person; Azuma is right-handed. Azuma's confession contained numerous false and improbable statements. Azuma was a poor student who would not have been able to write the elaborate confession police released to the media.

One possibility is that Azuma wrote the letter to the newspaper, but didn't commit the murder. He might have been trying to gain notoriety by taking responsibility for somebody else's crime. Another problem is that a police investigator might have written the confession based on statements Azuma made in custody.

He Walked Free

There is one more similarity to Graham Young's case; on March 11, 2004, the Kobe killer walked out of a reformatory school near Tokyo. A parole board had approved his release. They noted that psychiatrists felt that Azuma had been rehabilitated and wanted to pay compensation to the families of his victims.

It isn't known where Azuma is today, although he is presumably living somewhere in Japan. Whether he is rehabilitated or not remains a question of debate; modern psychology and historic cases indicate that psychopaths cannot be rehabilitated. Instead, they learn how to go along with society's rules out of a sense of self-interest rather than reform. If this is the case, the Japanese authorities might have released a serial killer, and whether he will kill again remains to be seen.

Bibliography

Blanco, Juan Ingacio. "Seito Skaibara ." n.d. muderpedia.rog . Online Encyclopedia Entry. 17 February 2013.

Japan Times . "Kobe killer set free ." 11 March 2004. murderpedia.org. Japan Times Newspaper Article . 17 February 2013.

Sharp, Johnny. "Graham Young, the St. Albans Poisoner ." n.d. trutv.com/library . Online Encyclopedia Entry. 16 February 2013.

Wikipedia . "Kobe child murders." n.d. en.wikipedia.org . Online encyclopedia entry. 17 February 2013.

—. "Zodiac Killer." n.d. en.wikipedia.org. Online Encyclopedia Entry. 17 February 2013.

Wikipedia. "Tsutomu Miyazaki." n.d. en.wikipedia.org. Online Encyclopedia Entry. 17 February 2013.

THE OUTRAGE THAT SHOCKED A NATION: THE MURDER OF JAMES BULGER

Introduction

Few crimes have attracted as much attention or generated as much outrage and fear as the abduction and murder of three-year-old James Bulger in 1993 by two ten-year-old boys. The crime shocked even the British, who are accustomed to horrifying crimes because of their sensational tabloid press.

Twenty years later the crime is still generating headlines and attracting vast amounts of media attention in Britain. The British people and their tabloids still cannot get enough of stories about the murder. Like Mary Bell's outrages in 1968, the case never seems to die or go away. Instead, the murder of James Bulger is as fresh in Britain's memory as it was when it was committed.

The Ten–Year-Old Child Killers

It's easy to see why the crime was so shocking; it was committed by two ten-year–old boys. Worse, it was committed in a public place closely watched by the closed circuit TV cameras that have become such a big part of British life in recent decades. For the first time, one of the world's most shocking crimes was caught on video tape for everybody to watch. To make matters worse, dozens of adults, who could have easily intervened and saved the boy, saw the abduction and did nothing to help.

The horror occurred on February 12, 1993, at the Bootle Strand Shopping Center, a mall in Liverpool. It began innocently enough with two young boys, Jon Venables and Robert Thompson, playing hooky, hanging out at the mall, and committing petty crimes, such as shoplifting. The day took a dark turn when Denise Bulger and her brother's girlfriend brought little James to the mall.

The crime occurred while Denise was in the butcher's shop and James was left to play outside. She got distracted when the butcher messed up her order, but her back was only turned for a minute. When she went back outside, James was gone. A mother's worst nightmare had come true, and it was about to get far worse.

Abducting and Killing a Toddler in Plain Sight

A desperate Denise Bulger flagged down a mall security officer and asked for help. Security announced the boy's disappearance over the building's loudspeakers while Denise and her friend Nicola frantically searched the shops for James. They were too late; Venables and

Thompson had already taken the boy out of the mall.

Once outside the building, the boys took James to a nearby canal and hit him. Then they inexplicably ran away from him. James started to cry and then, not knowing any better, followed the young sociopaths. Even though they took the boy down a crowded street where dozens of pedestrians and motorists saw them, nobody intervened. One witness even saw Thompson kick James in the ribs.

The two boys eventually picked James up and carried him to an empty field near a pond. On the way, at least two people saw the three boys, and neither of them helped even though one actually saw Venables punch James. An elderly woman came over and asked if anything was wrong. She told the boys to go to the police, but they ignored her.

That's right; several people had a close look at the abduction, and nobody tried to stop it. Venables and Thompson dragged James for at least two miles through a crowded city. The boy was even hurt and bleeding, but nobody helped. At one point, they even went into a store and bought candy for their younger brother. The boys also went into a pet shop and watched firefighters fight a fire. Incredibly, the only people who tried to intervene were two older boys, who told them to take James home.

The Murder at the Railroad Tracks

After taking James through town, Venables and Thompson took him to an isolated spot on some railroad tracks. Once there, for unusual reasons, they painted James' face then beat him with bricks and an iron bar. The boys also pulled off James' pants and probably sexually assaulted him. They finally fled when a train passed by. The train may have done the actual work of killing because the boys had laid James on the track so a passing train would tear him in two.

Incredibly, the scene of the murder was only a short distance from a police station. The police had been investigating James Bulger's disappearance for nearly two hours when he was killed. Investigators estimated that the murder occurred between 4:45 and 6:30 p.m. Denise Bulger had called the police around 4:15 p.m.

Unfortunately the police were on the wrong track; alerted by the witnesses who had seen James at the canal, they had divers search the water there. A more successful method was to put pictures of the abductors on TV, which they did. Constables had spotted Venables and

Thompson on the surveillance video from the mall.

It wasn't until Sunday morning, nearly two days later, that a train driver (engineer, in America) spotted something on the tracks. The driver thought it was a doll dumped on the track and ignored it. On Sunday afternoon four boys playing near the tracks found James' body.

A Savage Crime Leads to Hysteria and a Witch Hunt

When police investigated, they discovered that a savage murder had occurred. Not only had James been ripped in two by a speeding train, but he had been injured 42 times. He had also been covered with bricks, and there were indications of sexual assault.

By the time the body was discovered, Britons already knew the awful truth that the horror had been perpetuated by two young boys. The surveillance tape of James' abduction was played all over the nation.

Hysteria Grips the City

One of those who saw the tape was Robert Thompson's mother, Ann, who asked him if he was the boy on the tape. Thompson lied to his mother and denied his involvement. Incredibly, Robert later brought a rose to a makeshift memorial near the murder scene.

Hysteria swept the Merseyside area of Liverpool, where the murder had occurred. The police received dozens of calls reporting boys as suspects, and an angry mob even attacked the home of a twelve-year-old suspect who had been questioned. Police caught a break when an anonymous caller mentioned Jon Venables and Robert Thompson and told detectives the two boys had been playing hooky at the time of the crime.

Deciding to check out the tip, police went to Robert Thompson's house and found that his shoes had blood on them. When constables went to pick up Jon Venables, they found he had blue paint on his coat. James Bulger's face had been covered with blue paint before the murder. Police were able to link Venables to the crime when his fingerprints were found in the store he and Robert had visited with James.

An Unparalleled Evil and Barbarity

Eventually, both Jon Venables and Robert Thompson admitted to it, then, like true psychopaths, each tried to blame the other for the crime. Jon and Robert were both charged with the abduction and murder and an attempt to abduct two other children from the mall.

It took over two years to prepare both boys for trial. Investigators had to conduct psychological examinations, and the courts had to make special preparations. The British court system wasn't prepared to deal with such young murderers. A special platform had to be built in the courtroom for the boys.

When the boys were finally sentenced on November 24, 1993, the judge called the murder "an unparalleled evil and barbarity." He also described the boys' conduct as "wicked and cunning." The sentence was that both boys be detained as long as Her Majesty's Secretary of State deemed them a threat to society.

Venables and Thompson Today

Two decades later the murder of James Bulger is still on the minds of the British people. Jon Venables and Robert Thompson were theoretically imprisoned for life but released and given new identities in 2001, an act that outraged James Bulger's parents.

In 2008 Jon Venables was arrested for downloading child pornography to his computer. Venables is currently back in prison for parole violation and will probably stay there. Robert Thompson is apparently a free man, living somewhere in the United Kingdom under an assumed name.

Two decades later the case lives on; James Bulger's father, Ralph, is planning to release a book about his late son called My James. The British tabloids regularly revisit the horror and James' parents. James' mother, Denise Fergus (who has since divorced and remarried), is campaigning in the media to keep Jon Venables, whom she describes a psychopath, in prison. Authorities seem to have agreed with her; news reports indicate that Venables will be held indefinitely for his own safety. Some crimes are so horrific that they never seem to die in the public imagination.

The case has claimed at least one more victim in recent years. In August 2012 the British press reported that 36-year-old Scott Bradley, a resident of Garlieston, Scotland, killed himself because local residents thought he was one of James Bulger's killers. News reports indicate that residents had been tormenting Bradley for months after rumors that he was actually Robert Thompson started circulating. There is no evidence that the rumors were true, but they claimed a life.

Bibliography

Baron, Alexander. "Op-Ed: Thompson & Venables are back in the news." 11 January 2012. digitaljournal.com. Digitial Journal Editorial. 13 February 2013.

Evans, Natalie. "A community in mourning 20 years on: Tragic James Bulger remembered on anniversary of his murder." 12 February 2013. mirror.co.uk/news. News Article from Mirror Newspaper. 13 February 2013.

Lawson, Helen. "Father killed himself after hate mob wrongly accused him of being James Bulger child killer Robert Thompson." 11 August 2012. dailymail.co.uk. Daily Mail newspaper article. 13 February 2013.

Masters, Brian. "Jon Venables is no longer the guilty boy who killed James Bulger." 4 March 2010. telegraph.co.uk. Telegragh Newspaper Article . 12 February 2013.

Scott, Shirley Lynn. "Death of James Bulger." n.d. trutv.com/library/crime. Online Encyclopedia Entry. 12 February 2013.

The Independent. "The Bulger Murder." 25 November 1993. independent.co.uk. Independent Newspaper Article. 13 February 2013.

THE KIPLAND KINKEL STORY: WAS HE INSPIRED BY A YEAR OF SCHOOL VIOLENCE

Introduction

The 1997-1998 School Year was a bloody time in America's schools. It saw four massacres in which students used guns to mow down their classmates. The most disturbing of the outrages was the last one, perpetuated by 15-year-old Kip Kinkel in Springfield, Ore. The shooting was frightening because parents, school administrators, police, psychologists, and other students had ample warning about Kinkel. He had even been arrested for bringing a stolen gun to school the day before the shooting. Yet he was never taken into custody and even allowed to return to his parents' home, where his father kept several high-powered guns after the arrest. Nobody, it seemed, wanted to believe that a white boy from a nice middle class family could be a time bomb waiting to go off.

A Terrible Lesson

A troubled 15-year-old named Kipland (or "Kip") Kinkel taught America's school administrators and law enforcement authorities a terrible lesson in 1998. Even though he was visibly violent, obviously troubled, obsessed with school shootings, and had access to guns, nobody made any serious effort to stop him.

What's really frightening is that Kip Kinkel even told a number of people that he wanted to commit a school shooting. He even expressed his admiration when he saw TV coverage of school shootings. Kinkel also had a history of violence; he had thrown rocks at moving cars in an attempt to run one off the road and hurt somebody.

Despite all of these signs, Kinkel was ignored, and worse, allowed to have access to guns. This neglect caused the deaths of Kin-

kel's parents and two of his high school classmates. It also led to the injuries of as many as a
dozen students at Thurston High School in
Springfield, Ore. on May 21, 1998.

An Upper Middle Class Childhood

Kipland Kinkel doesn't fit the popular image
of a violent, troubled teenager. He came from
a white upper middle class family. His parents
could afford to spend a year in Spain and vaca-
tion in Hawaii when he was boy. There were no
visible signs of abuse or neglect in the affluent
family.

Despite his family's comfortable position,
Kip Kinkel began to have trouble in school. Like
many violent children, Kinkel began to exhibit
two very different sides to his personality. In
fourth grade, Kip was diagnosed with a learn-
ing disability and sent to a special education

program. At the same time, he was placed in a gifted and talented program.

By the time he was in the seventh grade, Kip was beginning to worry some of his teachers. He reportedly tried to order a bomb-making manual called The Anarchist's Cookbook online. In eighth grade, Kip got caught stealing CDs from Target and he bought a sawed-off shotgun from a friend.

From Troubled Kid to Violent Teen

The year 1997 was a turning point for Kip Kinkel. He exhibited his first signs of violence. He also learned about school shootings and had his first experiences with the mental health system.

Kip was arrested in 1997 when he and a friend dropped rocks onto cars from a highway overpass in Bend, Ore. Kip tried to blame his friend for the incident and show regret, but he ended up in the juvenile justice system anyway.

Kip's parents, Faith and Bill Kinkel, turned to psychologist Dr. Jeffrey Hicks for help. Faith told Hicks she was worried that Kip would hurt others and admitted she was afraid that he would hurt somebody. The psychologist apparently didn't help very much, and Kip actually got worse and became depressed.

When Dr. John Crumbley, a psychologist for the Oregon Department of Youth Services, assessed Kip as an investigation of the rock throwing incident, he was impressed by the Kinkels. Crumbley felt Kip was remorseful and recommended that he receive 32 hours of community service.

Psychology Fails to Help

Even though Dr. Hicks reported that his therapy sessions were helpful to Kip, the boy didn't improve. It apparently got worse; Kip was suspended from school twice for violent attacks on other students. Faith Kinkel also claimed her son's behavior was getting better.

It seems that Kinkel was exhibiting classic sociopathic behavior, showing authority figures and counselors what they wanted to see, while continuing his wrongdoing out of their sight. Hicks finally admitted the therapy had failed on June 2, 1997, and he prescribed the psychiatric medication Prozac to Kip.

Prozac has been linked to other violent children, including Edward Belben, a 15-year-boy in England who beat and stabbed his father to death. Belben also tried to kill his mother by stabbing her in the face with a pair of scissors.

Alyssa Bustamante was reportedly taking Prozac when she slit the throat of a nine-year-old girl in Tennessee.

Returning to High School for a Year of Violence

Dr. Hicks felt Kinkel was doing well and felt there were no problems. The doctor was very wrong; Kip wasn't doing very well, and at the same time Hicks said Kinkel was doing better, the boy bought a pistol from a friend.

Despite his problems, Kinkel entered Thurston High School for his freshman year. It was 1997, the beginning of a year of violence in America's schools. Sometime in the fall of 1997, Kip Kinkel went off Proazc. He also stunned classmates by giving a speech in class on how to make a bomb.

High profile school shootings in Pearl, Miss., and West Paducah, Kentucky, made the news and a big impression on Kip Kinkel. In March 24, 1998, there was another school shooting at Jonesboro, Ark. In that incident, Mitchell Johnson and Andrew Golden killed five people and injured ten. When Kip saw the coverage of the massacre on TV, he expressed admiration for the shooters.

The Police Knew about Kip and Did Nothing

The Jonesboro slaughter marked the beginning of a spiral of self-destructive violence for Kip Kinkel. He became more and more violent and uncontrollable. His behavior ranged from ordinary teenaged pranks, such as toilet papering a neighbor's house, to disturbing, such as purchasing stolen guns.

Incredibly, police became aware of the fact that Kip Kinkel was buying stolen guns and storing them in his locker at high school, but they did little at this time. On May, 20 1998, Detective Al Warthen discovered that Kip had a stolen Beretta semiautomatic pistol in his locker. Kip and another boy, Korey Ewert, were arrested for the crime and expelled from school.

Instead of going to juvenile hall or a psychological evaluation, Kip Kinkel was released into his father's custody, even though he had committed a felony. The violent and troubled boy was sent home. The home contained a number of guns, including a 22 rifle that Kip kept in his room. Bill Kinkel had bought Kip the rifle during the fall.

The Massacre Took Less than a Minute

The first thing Kip Kinkel did when he got home was shoot his father through the head with the rifle he had been given as a present. Kip then waited at home until his mother came home; he told Faith that he loved her, and then shot her six times. Twice in the back of the head, three times in the face, and once in the heart.

The next day, May 21, 1998, Kip went back to Thurston High School. He brought a backpack filled with ammunition, a semiautomatic rifle, a 9 mm Glock automatic pistol, and a .22 caliber Ruger semiautomatic pistol with him.

As soon as he entered the school, Kip started gunning down his classmates. After shooting two boys in the hall, he entered the cafeteria and fired 50 rounds from the rifle into students gathered for breakfast. He also managed to fire at least one round from the Glock before five classmates pounced on him and wrestled him to the ground.

Kinkel's shooting rampage took only a minute, but when it ended, two students were dead and 25 were injured. Police, including Detective Warthen, arrived on the scene and took Kinkel to the police station. They failed to search Kinkel, who had a hunting knife taped to his leg. When they reached the police station, Kinkel tried to stab Warthen with the knife, but failed.

In Prison and on Appeal

Kip Kinkel pleaded guilty to murder and assault with a firearm on Nov. 2, 1999. He was sentenced to 111 years in prison, but his sentence is still under appeal. Kinkel was held in the MacLaren Youth Correctional Facility, where he received treatment for his mental problems until he was 24. Kinkel was later transferred to an adult prison.

Since 1999, his attorneys have been appealing his sentence because they feel he was mentally ill and incapable of standing trial when he pleaded guilty. Kinkel reportedly wants to be transferred to a state mental hospital. In 2011, appeals in state courts were exhausted, but media reports indicate Kinkel is still continuing to appeal in federal court. If the appeals fail, Kinkel will probably stay in prison for the rest of his life; the earliest date he could be released is in January 2011.

Good Came Out of It

Some good did come out of Kip Kinkel's rampage and similar crimes. Police now respond aggressively to reports of planned

school shootings and take suspects into custo-

dy. School authorities now report signs of vio-

lent behavior to authorities.

Bibliography

Adams, Mike. "After Taking Prozac, Teen Beats Father to Death with Hammer ." 9 February 2009. naturalnews.com . Blog Entry . 14 February 2013.

Bacon, Brittany. "School Shooter Kip Kinkel Wants his Day in Court." 19 June 2007. abcnews.go.com . ABC News Article . 15 Febraury 2013.

Bernstein, Mazine. "Kip Kinke. convicted in Thurston High shooting wants to go to state mental hospital." 11 August 2011. oregnlive.com . Oregonian newspaper article . 15 February 2013.

Blanco, Juan Ignacio. "Barry Dale Loukaitis
." n.d. murderpedia.org . Online Encyclopedia
Entry and Compilation of News Articles . 14
February 2013.

CBS News Staff. "Alyssa Bustamante Picture
Gallery at 48 Hours website ." n.d.
cbsnews.com. Online Picture Gallery and
Commentary . 13 February 2013.

drugs.com. "Prozac ." n.d. drugs.com .
Online Database Entry . 13 February 2013.

Friesen, Mark. "The suspect: Kipland Kin-
kel's dark side was no secret to his peers." 22
May 1998. oregonlive.com . The Orgegonian
Newspaper Article . 15 February 2013.

Mcaffee.cc. "Profile of the Sociopath." n.d. mcafee.cc . Online Database Entry. 15 February 2013.

PBS Frontline Staff . "Who is Kip Kinkel ." n.d. pbs.org/wgbh. Chronology of Kip Kinkel's Life and Crimes . 15 February 2013.

Salem-News. "Thurston Shooter Kip Kinkel Transferred to Oregon State Prison ." 11 June 1 2007. salem-news.com. Salem News Newspaper Article . 15 February 2013.

The History Channel. "A school shooting in Jonesboro, Akransas, kills five ." 24 March 1998. history.com/this-day-in-history. This day in history feature from History.com . 15 February 2013.

CINDY COLLIER AND SHIRLEY WOLF: THRILL KILLING RUNAWAYS

Introduction

Young girls are less likely to kill than boys, but when they do, it is often far more frightening. Girls who kill are more likely to target strangers and those who cannot fight back, such as children and the elderly. Mary Bell killed two young boys in Newcastle, England in 1968, and Alyssa Bustamante slit the throat of a nine-year-old neighbor. Even more disturbing is the case of Cindy Collier, 15, and Shirley Wolf, 14. The two girls picked out an elderly woman at random and stabbed her to death for the fun of it. The case was made all the more frightening by the fact that they killed the woman in her own home.

Killing an Old Lady was Lots of Fun

Despite their innocent nickname, the "Little Girls Lost" teenagers, Cindy Collier and Shirley Wolf were a pair of thrill-killing monsters. They deliberately sought out an 86-year-old grandmother and stabbed her to death in order to steal her car.

The most frightening aspect of the crime is that 14-year-old Shirley and 15-year-old Cindy seem to have thought up the idea on the spur of the moment. The two girls had reportedly met only eight hours before, yet they felt confident enough to seek out an elderly lady they didn't even know and savagely murder her. The horror was compounded by the following words that Shirley wrote in her diary:

"Today, Cindy and I ran away and killed an old lady. It was lots of fun."

From Lost Girls to Cold-Blooded Murderers

Cindy Collier and Shirley Wolf had a lot in common. Both were juvenile offenders from dysfunctional families. Both had reportedly been sexually abused when they were younger.

Shirley Wolf's family background was made worse by the fact that her father was a registered sexual offender. He had been convicted of molesting Shirley since she was three years old.

By age 12, Cindy Collier had so many run-ins with the law that she could quote the Miranda warning police officers read during arrests by memory. Charges against Cindy included assault, burglary, and theft. Not surprisingly, Cindy was a regular guest at Juvenile Hall in Auburn, Calif. where she lived. Cindy also had a reputation for being violent and aggressive and attacking other students in high school.

The two girls apparently met at a group home where authorities had sent Shirley to protect her from her father. They decided to run away from Auburn, Calif., the town outside Sacramento where they were living, but realized they'd need a car to do it. It was that plan to get away from their boring and abusive environment that led them to murder.

Stabbing a Grandmother to Death

The horror unfolded on June 14, 1983 at the Auburn Greens, a condominium development where many senior citizens lived. Collier and Wolf went there because they decided that an old lady would be easier to rob and murder. The girls went door to door and pretended to ask for directions and water.

Most of the residents didn't let them in, but Joe Becker and his wife did. When the couple talked to the girls, they became frightened and disturbed. The girls left, but Mrs. Becker responded to their presence by scrubbing the telephone with alcohol because she felt it had been contaminated by their evil.

Eventually, 86-year-old Anna Brackett, a kindly retired seamstress and grandmother, let the girls in. They chatted with her for an hour, and whether this was to get Mrs. Brackett off-guard or simply because they were scared is not known. Eventually, Mrs. Brackett got a phone call from her son, who was coming over to pick her up.

When they heard that a man was coming over, the girls acted. They stole a knife from the kitchen and used it to stab the woman. Reports indicate that Wolf did the stabbing. After the stabbing, Collier ransacked the condominium and found the keys to a 1970 Dodge. Brackett kept the car parked in the condo's garage.

Nobody Suspected the Girls

The old Dodge in the garage did not start, so the girls decided to hitchhike home. Incredibly, Anna Brackett's son, Carl, passed them on the way to pick up his mother. At his mother's home, Carl discovered a scene that reminded him of the movie Psycho: his mother had been stabbed 28 times.

Neither Carl Brackett nor the Sheriff's deputies that responded to the crime scene could believe two teenaged girls committed the crime. Instead, suspicions fell upon an escaped patient from a local hospital. After detectives investigated and learned that 11 people had seen the girls at the condominiums, they decided to investigate.

Deputies went to Collier's home and found her and Wolf there asleep. When they woke up, Wolf confessed to the crime while Collier remained silent. When confronted, Collier laughed and said she wanted to kill someone just for fun.

A Short Time in Prison

Even though both Shirley Wolf and Cindy Collier were found guilty of first degree murder, they would each spend less than 12 years in juvenile facilities and prison. The reason for the short sentences was that the two were tried as juveniles, rather than adults, which limited their potential sentences.

The two women apparently went very different directions in the prison system. Cindy Collier seems to have reformed, even though she was a more hardened criminal. Collier reportedly got her junior college degree in the California Authority Facility where she was housed. Since being paroled in 1992, Collier has reportedly married and had four children. Some rumors indicate that she might be living in Auburn, Calif. again.

Wolf has reportedly been in and out of jail several times since being paroled from the Central California Women's facility in 1995. Her crimes reportedly include prostitution and an assault. There is no evidence that Wolf and Collier have had any contact since their trial.

The Case Never Seems to Die

Although Wolf and Collier have kept a low profile, their crime continues to attract attention. Author Joan Merriam published a book about the two called Little Girl Lost in 1992. Merriam believes abuse and neglect drove the two to murder Brackett. Since then, it has been the focus of numerous media outlets. Collier and Wolf were featured on an episode of the

Australian-American TV documentary series Deadly Women, which has been broadcast on the Discovery Channel and its sister networks in the U.S. The case never seems to go away, even if the murderers seem to have moved on.

Bibliography

Fenske, Sarah. "Alyssa Bustamante: Prosecutors Can't Use Part of Killer Teen's Confession." 23 June 2011. blogs.riverfronttimes.com . Online News Blog . 13 February 2013.

Khokhobashvili, Krissi. "Auburn's 'baby-faced killers' featured on Investigation Discovery ." 29 December 2011. auburnjournal.com. Auburn Journal Newspaper Article . 14 February 2013.

McCall, Cheryl. "A Grandmother is Murdered, Two Teenaged Girls are Convicted - There the Questions Begin." 29 August 1983. people.com/people/archive . People Magazine Article . 15 February 2013.

Murder UK. "Mary Bell Fact File ." 2011.
www.murderuk.com/child_killers. Online Fact
File . 12 February 2013.

Wikipedia . "List of Deadly Women epsiodes
." n.d. en.wikipedia.org. Online Encyclopedia
Entry . 14 February 2013.

WILLIE BOSKET: THE MONSTER WHO INSPIRED A LAW

Introduction

Traditionally, juvenile law is based upon the premise that all children and teenagers can be reformed into good citizens. Unfortunately, history has shown that isn't always the case; some killer kids are just so violent and out of control that little can be done for them. This lesson was a hard one for the American justice system to learn. It took the violent rampage of a second-generation predator known as Willie Bosket and the deaths of two innocent subway passengers to get politicians to give prosecutors the tools they needed to deal with such monsters.

The Killer Kid who Changed American Justice

Perhaps no killer kid has ever developed the reputation of 15-year-old Willie Bosket. Bosket's actions were so violent and frightening that they inspired the state of New York to amend a longstanding law. Bosket, who proudly calls himself a monster, was later listed as the most violent inmate in New York's state prison system. That's saying a lot because that system is one of America's largest.

Despite his funny name, Willie Bosket was a very violent young man. He reportedly committed 2,000 crimes before the age of 15, including 25 stabbings. Yet astoundingly, he was left out on the streets of New York City and allowed to have contact with his mother's boyfriend, a hardened criminal who sold Willie a gun.

Like Father, Like Son

By the time he was 15, Willie Bosket was a predator who roamed New York's subway system and preyed on its passengers. The time was the late 1970s, one of the most violent periods in the history of America's largest city.

Street crime was out of control and police were undermanned and underfunded. It was a perfect environment for a hardened mugger and thief like Willie Bosket.

Bosket was a poor, young African-American boy from Harlem who grew up in a very bad family. His father, William James Bosket Sr., was also a hardened professional criminal who spent time in the same reform school that Willie later attended. William Bosket was a double murderer, prison escapee, and bank robber who eventually made the FBI's Most Wanted List.

Willie Bosket was hardly a normal young boy, yet juvenile authorities treated him as just that. They let him out onto the streets where he stole purses and mugged passengers on the subway. Some accounts indicate that Bosket was even being considered for adoption by a

"good" family when he turned the subways into a killing ground.

From Subway Predator to Murderer

By March 19, 1978, Willie Bosket was roam-
ing the subways with a loaded handgun. On
that day, he found Noel Perez, a middle-aged
passenger who reminded him of a counselor at
reform school. Bosket shot Perez twice and
stole his watch. Some reports indicate that Willie Bosket was enraged at Perez because he
was wearing glasses that were similar to those
worn by a hated camp counselor.

Willie then committed a series of subway
robberies that included the shooting and robbery of a subway motorman. He and his cousin,
Herman Spates, also kicked a man down the
steps of a subway station in order to steal $12
from him. During their crime spree, Willie was

actually stopped by transit police, but let go because he looked young.

Eventually, Willie shot and killed a subway passenger named Moises Perez (no relation to Noel) because the unlucky man had no money. On the same day, the New York Division for Youth gave a final approval for Willie to be adopted.

The Laws Enabled the Violent Monster

The investigation of the Moises Perez shooting led NYPD homicide detective Martin Davin to Willie Bosket and Herman Spates. Davin was able to put pressure on Herman and force him to rat out Bosket.

Even though Davin gave prosecutors a strong case against Willie Bosket, there was little they could do to him. At the time, New York's laws limited the maximum sentence for violent juvenile offenders, including murderers, to 18 months. The idea was that most juvenile offenders could be reformed with the right environment. The problem was that Willie Bosket wasn't like most juvenile offenders. He was violent and aggressive, and he even boasted of his plans to kill somebody to counselors. Bosket said he wanted to be a killer just like his father.

Part of the problem was that in 1978, Willie Bosket was sent to family court, not criminal court. All family court could do with Willie was turn him over to the Division of Youth, which could only hold him for six years and had to turn him loose when he turned 21.

The Monster Changes the Law

Willie Bosket's case attracted even more attention because 1978 was an election year in the state of New York. The public was sick and tired of rampant crime and demanding action. Bosket's heinous actions were what finally forced politicians to take drastic action and change American criminal justice forever.

Governor Hugh Carey, who was facing re-election, called a special session of the state legislature. The legislature passed the Juvenile Offender Act of 1978, which allowed select juvenile offenders as young as 13 to be tried as adults. The Act was a radical break with the traditions of American law that noted that all teenagers and children could be rehabilitated.

The politicians had realized that some children were just so violent and out of control that the juvenile authorities couldn't deal with them. Those kids, like some adults, would have to be locked up to prevent further violence and harm to others. The law became a model for other states and was even known as the Willie Bosket Law.

He Walked Free Again

Ironically enough, Willie Bosket was not covered by the law that bore his name. He served four years in the Division of Youth and was released at age 21, just as the authorities had feared.

Interestingly enough, Bosket next tried to reform; he enrolled in community college, started looking for a job, and announced his plans to marry his girlfriend. The reform ended when Willie was arrested for mugging a 72-year-old man. Bosket was back in the court system, but his criminal record couldn't be used against him because he committed crimes as a juvenile.

Bosket's next crime was probably his stupidest; he got into a fight with bailiffs in the court room where he was on trial for assault. Not surprisingly, the court gave him little leniency; he was convicted of assault, resisting arrest, and contempt of court.

The Most Violent Prisoner in New York State

When he finally reached adult prison, Willie Bosket quickly developed a reputation as the most violent prisoner in the state of New York. His crimes behind bars have included arson, several escape attempts, and nine attacks on guards. He was eventually convicted twice and sentenced to 53 years to life.

Willie Bosket was so violent and uncontrollable that prison authorities placed him in solitary confinement for 20 years. His violence made him a monster and a legend. In 1988, Bosket was moved to a special Plexiglas cell, with four video cameras watching him at all times. Bosket is not allowed to speak to guards, and he has nothing in his cell but a cot and a toilet because he is so violent.

Disturbingly enough, Willie Bosket is regarded as a hero by some African-American men who see him as the victim of racism. In reality, Willie Bosket is probably the victim of his own uncontrollable violence.

Bosket is still in the New York State prison system and will remain there. He will also remain in solitary confinement, and some news stories indicate that under the current rules, Bosket might stay in solitary until 2046. Even if he gets out of solitary, Willie Bosket will have little to look forward to in his life; he is not eligible for parole until 2062 when he will be 100

years old.

Bibliography

Butterfield, Fox. "A Boy Killed Coldly is Now a Prison 'Monster'." 22 March 1989. nytimes.com. New York Times Feature Article . 16 February 2013.

The Anti. "Willie Bosket ." 10 January 2011. msexceptiontotherule.wordpress.com. Blog Entry. 16 February 2013.

W.E.A.L.B.E. "Willie Bosket: The Most Dangerous Prisoner in Amerikka." 28 April 2006. weallbe.blogspot.com. Blog Entry. 16 February 2013.

Wikipedia . "Willie Bosket ." n.d. en.wikipedia.org. Online Encyclopedia Entry. 16 February 2014.

READY FOR MORE?

We hope you enjoyed reading this series. If you are ready to read similar stories, check out other books in the *Murder and Mayhem* series:

America's First Serial Killers: A Biography of the Harpe Brothers (By Wallace Edwards)
They murdered. They stole. And they did it all to excess. Unlike other bandits of early America, they didn't do it for the money--they did it for the thrill and love of blood. They were the Harpe Brothers, and they have been called America's first true serial killers.

In this gripping narrative, the crimes and the lives of America's most notorious sibling killers are documented like a page-turning novel.

Deadly Darlings: The Horrifying True Accounts of Children Turned Into Murderers (By William Webb)

If you've ever thought your child was bad, then you haven't seen anything yet! In the pages that follow, you are about to meet some of the most vicious children who ever lived.

The kids in this book are as young as ten-years-old and they are ruthless. The nice ones killed in cold blood—but many of these kids weren't nice...they wanted their victims to suffer.

Some were turned killers by their brutal home environments; others were just inherently evil.

They were all deadly darlings you'd never want to meet on the street.

The Teacup Poisoner: A Biography of Serial Killer Graham Young (By Fergus Mason)

Graham Young had an unusual obsession from a young age. Where most youths might be interested in music and sports, Young was fascinated by poisons. By the age of 14, he was using his family (who, of course, didn't know) as experiments. In 1962, still a teen, his stepmother died from one of his poisoning experiments.

Young eventually confessed to the murder of his stepmother and the attempted murder of several other members of his family; he was sent to a mental hospital for nine years, where he was ultimately released fully recovered. Unknown to the hospital, however, Young was actually using his time in the mental hospital to study medical texts and improve his poisoning skills. His true work as a poisoner had only just begun!

This gripping narrative gives you a page-turning look at one of England's most notorious serial killers: Graham Young.

The Butcher Baker: The Search for Alaskan Serial Killer Robert Hansen (By Reagan Martin)
Beautiful Alaska--a peaceful, natural land where you know your neighbors and don't have to lock your doors. For most people, it's the perfect place to experience nature; for Robert Hansen, it was the perfect place for murder.

Between 1980 and 1983, Hansen went on a murderous rampage killing between 17 and 37 women in the Anchorage, Alaska area. Hansen, a small-business owner, and pillar of the community was also an avid hunter and used young girls as prey when he decided he needed a more challenging hunt.

This book is the gripping account of the hunt and eventual capture of an unlikely killer, who almost got away with it.

Mary Cecilia Rogers and the Real Life Inspiration of Edgar Allan Poe's Marie Roget (By Wallace Edwards)

The murder of Mary Rogers may not be well known today, but in the 19th century, it was one of the most compelling murders of the century. It became a national sensation--so much so that Edgar Allan Poe used it as the inspiration for his story "The Mystery of Marie Roget."

This chilling narrative will take you back in time to 1838, where you will learn the details of the case and how it became a national phenomenon.

Miscarriage of Justice: The Murder of Teresa de Simone (By Fergus Mason)

The murder was brutal--raped and strangled. The case was open and shut--a man had confessed to the murder, and he was easily convicted. There was a problem with the man's testimony, however...he was a pathological liar who had confessed to over 200 other crimes--many of which never happened.

For over 27 years, Sean Hodgson, the convicted murderer, sat in prison for a crime he didn't commit. The real killer, 17-year-old David Lace, had also confessed to the crime, but police didn't believe him.

This gripping short book takes the reader on the hunt for the real killer and reveals the creation of Operation Iceberg--the operation that led to the DNA review of over 240 other convictions.

No Guns Allowed On Casual Friday: 15 Of the Scariest Co-Workers You Will Never Want to Work With (By William Webb)

Almost everyone thinks it: "One day I'm going to give my boss what he has coming." The fifteen people in this book took this notion to the extreme.

What kind of workplace drives a person into performing such heinous acts? Does a workplace drive a person to kill, or is the killer already inside, waiting for a reason to act out? Find out in this fascinating quick read.

If you are stressed at work, then maybe this book will show you that you don't have it so bad; or maybe it will show you that the person in the cubicle next to you may need to be handled a little more...delicately.

NEWSLETTER OFFER

Don't forget to sign up for your newsletter to grab your free book:

http://www.absolutecrime.com/newsletter

www.ingramcontent.com/pod-product-compliance
Lightning Source LLC
Chambersburg PA
CBHW051343280526
45784CB00007B/2800